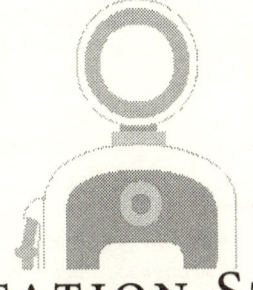

GAS STATION STORIES

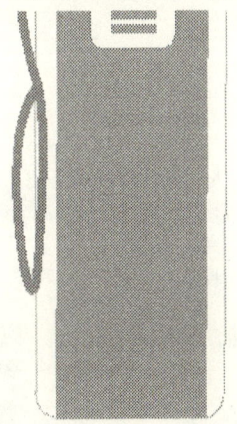

BOB BALCH

Bloomington, IN  Milton Keynes, UK

authorHOUSE®

AuthorHouse™
1663 Liberty Drive, Suite 200
Bloomington, IN 47403
www.authorhouse.com
Phone: 1-800-839-8640

This book is a work of non-fiction. Unless otherwise noted, the author
and the publisher make no explicit guarantees as to the accuracy of
the information contained in this book and in some cases, names
of people and places have been altered to protect their privacy.

First published by AuthorHouse 5/16/2007

ISBN: 978-1-4343-1171-9 (sc)

Printed in the United States of America
Bloomington, Indiana

This book is printed on acid-free paper.

This book is a work of nonfiction. Places, events, and situations in this
story have some truth in fact, and any resemblance to actual persons,
living or dead, is intended as these folks are an integral part of the story
and hopefully will bring some enjoyment to them or their families as they
reminisce about these times and events.

DEDICATION

THIS BOOK IS DEDICATED TO all of my friends and family who contributed their ideas, stories, and memories for me to draw upon in writing this book. Hopefully, with their help you will get a glimpse of "Americana" of the mid 20th century that will make you laugh, maybe shed a tear or two, and finally, long for that more simple but satisfying life we led in this country after World War II.

Bob Balch
8/5/04

"THE COVER"

I saw my friend and Justice of the Peace for Baylor County, Charles Thomas Sessions, at the Courthouse in Seymour, Texas, yesterday, and he told me a story about Frank Keck, the Texaco consignee for Seymour and the surrounding area for many years. He also said that he had some photographs at his station that I should look at so we met at the station on the Lubbock Highway at the Southwest corner of California and Foley Streets a little while later. I went to high school in Seymour with Charles Thomas who was a class ahead of me, and he is married to my friend and classmate, Sandra Henshaw Sessions. Stepping inside the station is like going back in time to the mid 50's where I observed the original lube lift and the old air compressor which still works. The station was built by Frank Keck in the 1950's, and his dad, Charles H. Sessions, took over its operation in October, 1955, according to a plaque on display in the old glass counter along with a lot of other Texaco memorabilia. The original station was a "Teague" design named after Walter Teague who began designing stations for Texaco in 1937. Later the station was remodeled using the "Matawan" design named after a station built in 1964 in Matawan, New Jersey, using sheet rock to cover most of the exterior walls.

The "Teague" design utilized a white porcelain tile for the exterior with red Texaco stars on the upper facades. Two service bays opening to the front for washing and marfak lubrication. Charles Thomas pulled the photographs out of the glass counter. The first showed the station as it appeared in 1958. You get a real life view of the station in operation. Look at the pumps with the globe displays on top of the "Sky Chief" which dispensed a premium fuel from the gray pumps, and the "Fire Chief" which dispensed regular gasoline out of the red pumps. See the oil displays on the gas island, and the upright coke box to the right of the front door. See the B.F. Goodrich tires and batteries sign at the right and the tire rack.

Charles Thomas then showed me a picture of what must be one of the oldest Texaco stations in Seymour gas station history. Located in the 200 block of N. Main on the east side of the street set this old rock structure. The two fellows in the picture are Frank and Walter Keck, brothers and the proprietors of this filling station. Note that the old pumps are on the curb right next to the highway. As you look at the picture, Frank is on the right, and he became the Texaco consignee for Seymour and the surrounding area. This picture was probably taken in the early 1920's. Note the various signs in the photograph. As to the story about Frank Keck, Charles Thomas related that one cold, snowy winter night,

Frank and his wife, Opal, were asleep in the second story of the old rock building which served as their home. Advertising Day or Night Service for Gas, Oil, and Accessories, a fellow and his female companion pulled up for service and made their presence known. Frank, after being awakened from his slumber, headed down stairs. The fellow said, "Give me five gallons of gas." Frank said something to the effect that "it's late at night, and you wake me up for only five gallons of gas." The man replied, "That's what I want only five gallons." The negotiations went back and forth, and finally the female traveling companion opened the door and said, "Fill 'er up before you decide to leave us on empty and go back to bed." Frank then smiled and pumped the tank full, which required first filling the glass globe at the top by pumping the gas for measurement, then dispensing the gas into the vehicle. This required some work, and you can see why Frank was reluctant to sell only five gallons to this stranger on this cold winter night. The old rock building is long gone, and Lawrence Brothers Grocery Store (formerly the M System) is located in this block.

Ole Frank Keck saw the evolution of the gas pump and station design from virtually the beginning of the business in the early days clear into the late 1970's. He finally sold his business to Nolan Davis and retired. Phil Davis and Brent Wardlaw now own the business.

I asked Charles Thomas if I could use these two photographs on the cover of my book entitled "Gas Station Stories," and he was happy to oblige me this honor. I hope you get as much enjoyment viewing these old photographs as I have. This kind of takes us full circle from "Spindletop" where Texaco was born, to the beginnings of commercial stations, to the great stations of the 1950's built after WWII. The reminiscence is complete. Thanks Charlie.

Bob Balch
12/13/06

TABLE OF CONTENTS

ACKNOWLEDGMENTS

I WANT TO THANK ALL of my friends for their input in helping me get the information for all of these stories. My mom, Modena Balch, was a great source of information, and she did some interviews for me to get the correct facts for these stories. She also remembers a story about a pet monkey owned by a carnival family which wintered in Mankins, Texas. It is said the monkey crossed the highway every day to a gas station whose operator gave him peanuts. Unfortunately, one day the unsuspecting monkey got hit by a truck and killed while crossing the highway. She claims there is a marker along side the road in memory of this beloved monkey which reads "Here lies the only monkey in the world who was killed by a truck while going to get peanuts." Needless to say, I'm in the process of checking out this story. My good friends Charles England Perry, Larry Cooper, Gary Southard, Ed Covington, James Rasmussen, John Arthur Underwood, and others who helped me with their ideas and memories. A special thanks to my friend and historian, Jack Jones, who provided a wealth of information which I have included in the book. Thanks to my fellow lawyer, Clifford Edwards, for his great story about filling up in Helena. A special thanks to my uncle, Carol Feemster,

for the information he provided and also his memories of Grandpa Roberson's station in Vera, Texas. Thanks to Cindy, Craig, Melody, and Marguerite McNeill for their remembrances. Thanks to Ralph Perkins for his remembrances about his uncle's station. Thanks to my Aunt Wanda Balch for her memories of her dad's station in Graham, Texas. Thanks to my cousin, Dr. Jim Balch, for the WWII information about my uncle and his dad, J. B. Balch. Thanks to Aubrey Ramsey for allowing me and Charles England Perry to interview him and write about his WWII experiences and growing up on a farm near Bonham, Texas. Also, to Charles England Perry for his story of Second Lieutenant R. G. Fraser in "Bombs Away." Thanks to Barbara Kafer for her story about the Hurnville Store. Thanks to Matt Gwinn for running my letter to the editor in the Baylor County Banner requesting information for this book. Thanks to Barbara Welch for the information about her dad, Cy, and the family station on lake road. Thanks to Graham Quisenberry for his response with information about his family's station, and to Hilda Kunkel for her story.
It seems that my letter in the Banner took her back a number of years and a trip to Wichita Falls. It had not rained for a long time, but on this particular day it was raining. She stopped to get gasoline. After filling her tank she ran into the station to make payment. Upon entering the station she exclaimed, "Isn't this wonderful weather!!?" The attendant replied, "For

ducks it is." To this day she wonders if that man is ever happy about anything.   Thanks again to my friend, John Underwood, for reviewing the final draft of the transcript for accuracy. Finally, thanks to all the people who lived these stories and which made this all possible for all of us to enjoy and remember.

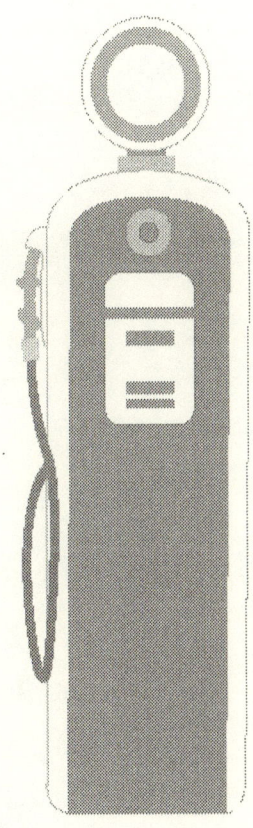

I.

"INTRODUCTION"

On a hot, late spring day in June, 2004, my good friend and fellow lawyer, Gary Southard, and I were just leaving a Texas Department of Corrections Unit outside of Beaumont, Texas, where we had been interviewing a client for a civil case we were working on at the time, when there off the road ahead was a sign pointing to Spindletop. Instinctively, we pulled off the highway and into the small park honoring one of the greatest oil discoveries in the history of both Texas and the nation. As we read the markers and looked out over the lake which now covered the collapsed dome, and the flag pole in the distance marking the spot of the first well, we were transported back in time to the year 1901. This was the birth of the great oil industry in Texas. Several major oil companies find their origins in this field. One bore the name of this great state, The Texas Oil Co., which changed its name to Texaco in 1959. Others included, Mobil, Gulf and Humble Oil. As we left Spindletop, I began to think about these companies and their logos, signs, and stations of the past so indelibly imprinted in the mind of my youth. I remembered back to my days growing up in Seymour, Texas, the cross-roads of five major highways, and the home of over fifty gas stations over the years. Seymour is a small North Texas town located on the Brazos River with a population of about 3,000 folks whose local economy depends primarily on farming, ranching, and to a lesser extent, oil and gas production. U.S. Highways 82, 277, 183, 283, and Texas Highway 114 cross here. With all of the traffic these highways accommodate it is no wonder that Seymour became a mecca for oil companies to sell their products. All of the majors competed for the business including Texaco, Mobil, Humble, Conoco, and Gulf. Others such as Phillips 66, Cosden, Panhandle, Bell, and Fina were represented. There were others in the earlier years. In the 50's there were stations all over Seymour. Most operators at the time leased their stations from the oil companies and agreed to sell their products by a franchise agreement. Their profits came on markups for gas and oil, for car washes and lubrication or "lube" jobs, and from service and repair work for their customers' vehicles. They also usually had small concessions where they sold candy, soft drinks, and knick-knacks. They also fixed flats and sold new tires, radiator hoses, batteries, and other small parts. All in all it was hard work but a gratifying life. It was certainly a fascinating place for a boy growing up in small town America to hang out.

The night before our visit to Spindletop, Gary Southard and I had spent the night with our friend Larry Cooper and his wife, Mary, in the Houston area. Larry is the cousin of Charles E. Perry, one of the lawyers in our group, and he grew up in Bells, Texas, went to Texas A&M, and then became an Ag teacher where he taught in several Texas public schools over the years. Now retired and living in Jersey Village, we had some good laughs when he told us about his experiences hanging out and working at a certain gas station in Bells. We'll learn more about that later. Larry is a walking history book as he tells story after story about life growing up in rural Texas in the 40's and 50's. We really enjoyed our visit and stayed up late into the night to listen to his exploits. As Gary and I traveled north on U.S. 287 through the Big Thicket, I got to thinking about all of the great times and funny incidents that occurred in the gas stations in Seymour where I hung out with my pals. As I told Gary some of these stories, I remembered that he had grown up in Midland, Texas, in another area of hot oil activity during the mid 20th century. In fact his dad worked for Marathon Oil Co. and also was a very successful lease hound. Gary promised me that he would add a few stories to the mix. Gary was Archer County Attorney for several years, and he reminded me of the Walsh Brothers Mobil Service Station at the Northwest corner of Texas Highways 79 and 25 on the courthouse square in Archer City, Texas. This place was an institution for half a century. The station opened in 1944 and was run by the Walsh brothers, Frank, Fred, Jay and Tom, who grew up in a large family from the Megargel community in Archer County. The old station finally closed in 1994. Known as the "Knowledge Corner," it was the favorite spot for locals to gather, visit, and solve the world's problems. The brothers are all deceased now, and the building was in a state of disrepair until the community and several organizations stepped in and saved it. Now completely restored and with the old gas pumps in front, it is a source of pride for the entire community and the North Texas area. Gary and I were in agreement that these are great memories. So the idea for this book was set in motion on that trip. Hopefully, it will recapture some of those good times for your enjoyment.

II.
"BRIEF HISTORY"

WITH THE ADVENT OF THE motor vehicle across America in the early 20th century, a new industry was born to service these so called "horseless carriages." When Henry Ford began to mass produce the Model T in 1908, the doors were opened for the average American to purchase a motor vehicle, and that they did in mass numbers. Gasoline was first sold behind the counter by local retailers such as hardware stores, grocery stores, general stores, blacksmiths, and garages which sprang up to repair these vehicles. It wasn't long before corporate America seized upon the opportunity to provide both service and gasoline, and the first American "filling stations" were born. As stated most fuels were sold in stores in cans without markers. In 1907 in St. Louis a small tin warehouse appeared with two high pedestals upon which rested two old metallic hot water tanks with ordinary garden nozzles from which a gravity flow system was used to dispense gasoline. According to "National Petroleum News" this was the first American gas station. From this humble beginning the first gas pumps began to appear on the scene with curbside service out of house like sheds. From purchasing gas by the bucket at first it now became necessary to measure sales uniformly by the gallon and pumps began to spring up that could do this for the proprietor and purchaser. Around 1910 stations resembling small houses with larger offices started to appear. Brand names, logos, and advertising arrived on the scene. In the middle teens standardized station designs appeared. In the 1920's for customer convenience canopies were added. In the 1930's bays began to appear offering repairs and other services. Other amenities such as public restrooms, water fountains, concessions, and even restaurants were provided. Slowly the station design evolved over time. A more uniform industrial type shape for full service appeared after WWII which continued until the explosion of the modern convenience store design with covered pumps clustered on islands throughout the large parking area in front of the stores in the early 1980's. The history of the development of the gas pump is a fascinating story in itself. Brand identification also was an important part of station layout and design as companies tried to get an advantage in the ever increasing market. From special identifying uniforms of the attendants to catchy slogans and mascots for their products, the advertising business never had it so good. Just close your eyes and think back in time. What do you see? Which slogans do you remember? Which mascots were your favorites? What were the colors, signs and logos of your favorite company? Now you are getting a feel for what this book is all about. Sit back and enjoy the ride.

III.
"WHY AMERICANS
ARE FASCINATED BY
GAS STATIONS"

WHEN I WAS ABOUT FIVE years old my parents gave me a model gas station with all the attachments. I thought it was the most beautiful thing that I had ever seen. From the model gasoline pumps, to the lifts in the bays, this was impressive. I admired the various colors, the signs and logos, and enjoyed moving the uniformed attendants to various locations in the layout. My friends and I would fill-up our various cars, trucks, jeeps, and other play vehicles, and perform various maintenance operations upon them at the station. This was great fun and entertainment for everyone. I kept this model for several years and never tired of playing with it.

Listening on the radio and then watching on television in the early 1950's, I knew every commercial and every company slogan by heart. One of my favorite treats was to ride to the station in the family automobile with my parents to "filler-up." I loved to watch the attendant check the oil, sweep out the floorboards, check the air pressure in the tires, and pump the gas. But, my favorite was watching the attendant check the water level in the radiator. This could be quite exciting, especially if the engine was hot. Various techniques were employed such as the cool down with the water hose method, or the wet rag technique with pressure applied to the cap. The fun started when the radiator started to blow steam and watching the actions of the attendant in the process. You get the drift. Finally, any trip to the gas station was not complete without a soda pop spiked with Tom's peanuts. What an outing, and what excitement for any kid.

On trips across country in the family automobile we would play a game of identification to pass the time. The object was for the first one to see the sought after item along the road to yell. The one who identified say 10 items first was the winner. You could use state license plates, makes and/or models of vehicles, or my favorite-brand name gas stations. I loved this game, and because I knew every company sign from a distance, was a very good player who was hard to beat. I won many a soda pop from my fellow travelers. Close your eyes. Can you see the signs? Gulf, Texaco, Mobil, Humble, Phillips 66, and on and on they come in the recesses of your memory.

On Saturdays during the fall of the year my ears were glued to my earphones attached to my transistor radio where Kern Tipps was broadcasting the Southwest

Conference Football Game of the Week for Humble Oil and Refining Company. He was the greatest announcer that I ever heard and could paint a picture in your minds eye on every play. We kids would replay the game in somebody's front yard and dream of playing someday when Kern Tipps would call out our names for our exploits on the field. We knew every Humble commercial played on those broadcasts. Their mascot was the tiger, and their slogan was "Let's put a Tiger in your tank." The nearest Humble station had a brochure to give you with every game listed including the date and time of the broadcast. What a treat. I can still hear Kern Tipps just like it was yesterday, and the little boy in me yearns for those days.

These are my stories, and every American has his or her own stories about their fascination with gas stations. But, all are proof positive of why we Americans are fascinated by this American institution.

IV.
"EVERYONE HAS MEMORIES OF THEIR FAVORITE STATIONS"

ASK ANY OF YOUR FRIENDS, stop a stranger, or inquire of your family members, and all will have memories and stories to tell about their favorite stations. You see, this is built into the psyche of all Americans. Nothing has been more liberating to the average American than his ability to own and operate his or her own motor vehicle which ushered into our lives such mobility that no destination was outside our reach. As the roadway system developed across this great nation, gas stations sprouted up everywhere to provide the fuel and services necessary to keep 'em running. Nothing seemed more inviting than that familiar oasis beside the road which provided what we needed to get us to our destination. For all of these reasons Americans have many fond memories of their favorite stations.

I asked my friend and historian, Jack Jones, to furnish me any information that he might have about fillin' stations in our hometown of Seymour, Texas. What arrived in the mail was a shocker because Jack had provided me with a narrative history of some 53 stations he remembered with their locations and operators. What a treat it was to visualize these stations and characters in my mind's eye. Jack also told me that one of his all time favorites was Grimes Garage in Hillsboro, Texas. Their slogan was "You wreck 'em, we pick 'em up." Jack often frequented this establishment in his travels from Seymour to Waco while attending Baylor University. That reminded me that my dad used to talk about Grimes Garage as we made our own trips to Waco and Baylor. Dad said that when he was hitchhiking back home that if he could only get to Grimes Garage that he would have no problem in getting a ride headed to Seymour. Jack Jones said there was a sign on top of Pikes Peak that read "Grimes Garage, Hillsboro, Texas. You wreck 'em, we pick 'em up." This place was well known and used unique early marketing techniques to establish its niche in the industry. On telling him this story, my friend and fellow Baylor lawyer, Jim Rasmussen, who grew up on a farm near Platte, South Dakota, and whose wife, Betty, worked for the establishment while they were dating, reminded me that Wall Drug founded in 1931 in Wall, South Dakota, near the Badlands, got famous by luring weary travelers with signs on the highways about the distance from Wall Drug for free ice water. He says that one of the astronauts even took a sign to the moon saying 243,000 miles to Wall Drug and pointing the way. That reminded me of the famous Burma Shave signs that you would see on the highways of America during the 50's. Each small sign spaced about fifty yards apart had a portion of the message which after reading about ten of them in a sequence would reveal the advertising message for the product. These were fun messages and very innovative advertising along the highways of America.

My all time favorite was Bill Boyd's Texaco right off the campus of Baylor University in Waco, Texas. I'll have more about this one later.

So, let's begin this sentimental journey as told by the people who garnered the memories of these favorite stations.

V.
"GRANDPA'S STATION"

MY GREAT GRANDPA ON MY mother's side was named William Franklin Roberson. Over his long and interesting life he wore my hats as a carpenter, school bus driver, farmer, and businessman. Will owned and operated a Gulf gas station in Vera, Texas, located about 20 miles west of Seymour on the Knox Prairie in Knox County, Texas. Vera was a thriving farming community on the path of U.S. 82 which was a two-lane dirt road in the 1920's from Seymour to Lubbock. Plans were approved in 1926, and the road was paved in 1930. My mom's brother, Garlin Feemster, and her dad's cousin, Uncle Bill Feemster, worked on this project. Garlin drove a gravel truck and Uncle Bill using a fresno (scoop) with teams of horses and mules dug the gravel from a pit near Gilliland, Texas.

During this time a stranger named Jim drifted into town and set up shop in the rear of Will Roberson's Gulf station as a mechanic. Grandpa gave him the run of the place, and Jim lived in the back. Jim proved to be a very good mechanic but evidently had a wild side as well. He loved to play cards and partake of the spirits. One day Jim came up missing, and Grandpa found blood splattered around in the shop. Grandpa reported his disappearance to the Knox County Sheriff. After conducting his investigation, the Sheriff knew that Jim had been involved in a heated card game in the back of the station where a lot of drinking was going on and tempers flared. Everybody's memory got real fuzzy at this point. The Sheriff searched several places and water wells but Jim's body was never found, and his disappearance went unsolved.

Grandpa drove the school bus from Vera to Benjamin during the school term. My mom rode that bus until she graduated from Benjamin High School in 1937. Grandpa never would let her drive that bus, but he sure was glad when she volunteered to help drive his old Model T from Vera to Ruidoso, New Mexico, for a family visit and vacation. Grandpa always tried to help his grandkids, and they loved him dearly. Whether it be fixing their bicycles or lending them money for a trip, he was always there with a helping hand. He was a very generous person and helped many people in need during the depression at his Gulf station.

Grandpa ran that Gulf station for several years. When his oldest daughter, Annie, and her husband, Walter Feemster, a grocery store owner, moved to Seymour, he soon followed and actually moved the home he had built in Vera to Seymour just down the street from his daughter. He and grandma, Luda Powell Roberson, always seemed to follow Annie. Grandpa sold the little Gulf station on the south side of the road, and it continued to serve the traveling public for several more years. The little station is no longer there, but I often think about it as I pass through Vera on U.S. 82 on my way to see my son, Josh, a student at Texas Tech University in Lubbock. It brings back memories of my Grandpa and the legacy he left to his family and friends and of his time spent serving the public at that little Gulf station on the roadway in rural America of the 1930's.

VI.
"MY FIRST MEMORIES OF GOING TO THE STATION"

I GREW UP ON NORTH Washington Street in Seymour just one-half block from all of the major highways winding their way through town. As a small pre school child of five my mother would allow me to walk south down the alley behind my house the ½ block to the intersection of Main and California Streets, where on the Northwest corner stood the J.T. Reeves Mobil station. It was a small frame building with hand operated pumps facing Main. There was no garage with bays for repairs. Mr. Reeves, a quiet elderly gentlemen, pumped gas, sold oil, serviced vehicles, and sold some grocery items, soft drinks, candy and miscellaneous concessions. His granddaughter, Mozelle Moore, reminded me that he used to keep clusters of bananas hanging inside the station for his customers. I loved to visit this tiny station. I felt so big and proud that mother would let me frequent this place without her presence. Mr. Reeves was always very polite to me and my friends and seemed to enjoy our frequent visits. We would drink soda pop, eat candy, and watch the world go by. Every once in a while Mr. Reeves would surprise me with a free treat. Sometimes he would let me sweep out the floorboards of his customers' vehicles. If my memory serves me correctly, he always wore a uniform and the company hat with the rounded top and small black bill. He ran a good business and had many regular customers. He also got good traffic flow. This was one of the best corners in town because all traffic headed west on U.S. 82 to Lubbock passed this intersection. Although having just one canopy and no bays, Mr. Reeves seemed content with what he offered and his niche in the gas business in Seymour in the late 40's and early 50's. As a small child it certainly made an impression on me. The little station is long gone and a Dairy Queen now sits on this site, but when I go home to visit my mom, I often walk down that alley and visualize that little station and can still see Mr. Reeves in my mind's eye waving for me to come on in for a visit.

VII.
"THE TEXACO STATION NEAR MY HOME"

WHILE GROWING UP IN SEYMOUR, Texas, I lived in a white stucco house built by my parents after World War II. Later, we moved across the street to the old Craddock house while my parents sold the old stucco house which was moved across town and prepared to build a new brick home on the premises. So, from 1947 thru 1965, until I left for college at Baylor, my domain was on North Washington Street within a half block of California Street (U.S. 82). At the Northwest corner of California and Washington stood a Texaco station. It was run by several operators down thru the years, including Walter Keck, Fred McCord, and Clarence Studer. Clarence Studer had two sons, Ralph and Tracy, who worked for their dad at the station. I began to hang out at this station on a regular basis. The emblem for Texaco was the red star. Their pitch was "Trust your car to the man who wears the star." Their emblem stood on a sign in front of the station. It had two bays one of which had a lift. I saw the first gasoline credit card machine in use at this station. You set the amount manually, laid the card in the track, put the paper charge slip in place then pushed the slide across which imprinted the card with the amount and the information off the card onto the charge slip, the hard copy being retained by the station for negotiation for payment, and the soft copy for the customer's records. I thought this was really something. This was the beginning of the great credit industry spawned from these early marketing techniques implemented by Texaco and other oil companies. You will remember that Texaco also began its long sponsorship of The New York Metropolitan Opera in 1940. In the 1960's they used T.V. advertising to market their products and pitchmen such as "Bob Hope." As a kid I was seeing all this evolve before me and had a ringside seat at the Texaco station just ½ block from my home on North Washington.

Let's get back to the Studer boys. Ralph was the oldest. Tracy was smaller than his brother but both were muscular in build and excellent athletes. Both played high school football for the Seymour Panthers. I used to love to go over there on Saturday mornings after the big game on Friday night and get their blow by blow descriptions of each play and laugh at their aches and pains. Looking back, you know, Clarence, their dad, and those two brothers were really tolerant of me and my friends. I know that I must have gotten in the way much of the time, but they never complained and always were glad to see me, well maybe most of the time.

I remember one particular day when we were really aggravating the brothers. Their dad wasn't around, and a lot of horseplay was going on inside the station. As I recollect, I got the water hose in the car wash bay and started spraying everybody in sight including the two brothers. The next thing I remember is that one of them got a length of rope and was chasing me as I ran toward the safety of my house. Before I could get home he caught me and wrapped the rope around me and pulled me back to the station. He tied my legs together and my hands behind me and hoisted me upside down up the trunk of a big ole Sycamore tree growing behind the station next to Washington street. I hung there upside down for nearly an hour. One of them tried to pour a soft drink into my mouth but I spewed it back at him. Every time one of my friends tried to get to me, the brothers would run them off. Boy, I really got 'em going that day. Finally, I guess one of them must have felt sorry for me because he came over and let me down. On reflection, the brothers probably were afraid that their dad might return to the station and discover what they were up too and let 'em have it. I told 'em that I'd get even, and I'm sure that I did but just can't remember the details. I do know that water guns, water balloons, pea shooters, and rubber guns were my weapons of choice in getting even and were at one time or another used against the Studer brothers. I was also not afraid to do certain things to their vehicles such as putting a dead fish or cat on the manifold, stuffing a potato up the tail pipe or using white shoe polish to leave certain messages. You get the drift. I guess those boys let us hang around because we would do some of their work for free such as pumping gas, sweeping floorboards, checking oil, radiators, and even washing cars. It was quid pro quo. Their deal was a free soda pop and candy if you'll cover for me for a while. Of course, I loved this and learned a lot about cars and their proper maintenance. As I grew up and Ralph then Tracy graduated from high school and moved on, I really missed them. Those were some great times.

VIII.
"AN EXPLOSIVE SITUATION"

My friend, Gary, told me about an incident he heard about that occurred in Midland, Texas, at a neighborhood gas station sometime in the 60's. It seems that a group of guys were cruising Midland with nothing in particular to do one evening when they stopped to use the rest room which the attendant had left unlocked at a station closed for the night. Just cruising the streets was a nightly ritual for teenagers growing up in America during the 60's. Midland at the time was a city of probably about 50,000 people and most were employed either directly or indirectly in the oil and gas industry which was the major revenue producer in the area. Gasoline was cheap and the automobile offered an escape for teenagers to hang out and the mobility to see a lot of people in a short time. Gas stations, drive-in restaurants with curb service, open area parking lots, drive in movies, and town squares were the favorite haunts of teenagers in those days. While cruising the streets that night in Midland, a pit stop was in order. One of the guys had a cherry bomb in his pocket and decided that if dropped lighted into the commode might cause quite an explosion. Cherry bombs are now illegal in Texas and most other jurisdictions but in the 60's were a favorite of teenagers because its waterproof fuse allowed it to explode under water. As you might imagine the cherry bomb on being lighted and flushed into the pipes with the delayed action did cause quite an explosion and caused quite a mess in the restroom and the plumbing for the station. Needless to say, the guys scattered like a bunch of surprised quail. It didn't take to long for the story to get out about this incident. The poor station owner was never able to determine who did the deed and nobody involved was talking. There were no doubt copy cat incidents at schools and other places. You can only imagine what kind of damage a cherry bomb could cause when exploded in a confined space under water. I remember throwing cherry bombs into the Brazos River as a kid and watching them explode. The explosion would make a "woosh" sound and send water high into the air. It's no wonder that they have been outlawed. Not to mention how dangerous they could be to the user. Well, so much for cherry bombs. Another favorite was the water balloon, and I'll talk about that in the next story.

IX.
"WATER BALLOON CAPERS"

An old Panhandle station was located at the southwest corner of California and Washington streets about a block from my house in Seymour, Texas. It faced the intersection diagonally. This location was also the distribution location for Panhandle. W.A. "Bun" Melear was the Panhandle agent and operator of the station. My friend, Jack Jones, said that a fellow named John Orsak worked for Bun and that "I can see him now, putting gasoline into a tank truck while puffing on a cigar. I waited and waited for an explosion, but it never did occur." Later, Robert Crowell operated the station. Then it was torn down and a new brick station was built on the site facing California street. It was directly across the Lubbock highway (California Street) from the Studer Texaco station which I discussed earlier in these stories. D.U. Cowart was the proprietor, and he had a son, Mike, who was a good friend and classmate. Behind this station and facing Washington Street stood Underwood Motor Company, the Pontiac dealership, owned by J.S. and Gertrude Underwood. Their son, John Arthur, was also my classmate and close friend growing up, and his family had moved from Vernon to

Seymour during his kindergarten years where I first met him in Miss Lois Drane's class. John Arthur worked at the dealership doing various jobs and naturally I frequented the place as well as "Ulley's" (D.U. Cowart's nickname) station next door. Mike worked at the station for his dad pumping gas, repairing tires, and other jobs. Loitering about these places guys like me, John Arthur, and Mike could think of a lot of mischievous things to do with our time. One of the favorite pranks was the water balloon capers. With such a strategic location there was plenty of traffic passing by on the way to Lubbock or local traffic in town. During Ulley's absence and while Mike was in charge, this location provided the perfect launching pad for balloons what with plenty of water and cover for hiding when hurling the balloons at the unsuspecting motorists passing by the station. One day we were practicing our accuracy by hurling balloons at the Studer boys across the highway at their station when we came upon the idea to use a rubber gun catapult to launch the balloons to provide extra speed and distance. This rubber gun catapult was made out of an old tire tube cut into lengths of about three feet each which were then attached to a metal frame and the other end to an old pillow case to hold the balloon before launching. Two guys would hold the metal frame and the other guy would put the water balloon in the pillow case and pull back hard, aim and fire. Wow! What a great tool. We launched a few high over the highway and couldn't believe the distance we were getting. Then we decided to aim for one of the Studer boy's vehicles parked beside the station across the street which sustained a direct hit, but fortunately did not bring a retaliation by the Studers. Next we decided to pick out certain vehicles traversing either Washington or California streets for a surprise attack. We could hide and launch at a distance so that the occupants of the passing vehicle had no idea where the attack originated. This approach worked well on unsuspecting girls and guys cruising around town. Unfortunately one of our water missiles hit an out of town traveling motorist on the windshield causing him to swerve and almost have a head on collision with oncoming highway traffic. This guy made the block and upon seeing Mike, John Arthur and me laughing and looking suspicious determined that we were the culprits. The local city police car just happened to be passing by and the traveler waved him over to the station. We had to fess up and apologize to the traveler and darn if the policeman didn't confiscate our rubber gun catapult. Well, it was fun while it lasted. I guess we should be thankful that no one got hurt. We then went back to the more conventional techniques of just throwing the balloons including the drive by attack which was popular while cruising the drag in Seymour. I guess some of the most fun I had growing up were the water balloon capers.

X.

"DUMP AND RUNT"

As I mentioned in the introduction, Larry Cooper, a friend of mine and cousin of my good friend, Charles England Perry, grew up in Bells, Texas, just a few miles east of Sherman. At the intersection of U. S. Highways 69 and 82 stood a fillin station operated by two guys we'll call Dump and Runt, which just happened to be their nicknames. Their station was the local gathering spot for all kinds of characters. I call these "spit and whittle clubs." Many of the world's problems are discussed and many a solution offered at gatherings of these little clubs at fillin stations, cafes, and coffee spots all over rural Texas even today. Besides Larry Cooper, who was a teenager at the time and spent many an hour working and sometimes just hanging out at the station, there were numerous characters who frequented Dump and Runt's station including a certain Colonel Foster, who liked the sauce, and one Pee Doodle, who wasn't carrying a full load if you get my drift. There was a good looking gal who ran a beer joint across the Red River in Oklahoma who was a frequent customer at the station. She liked to wear tight shorts. One day Colonel Foster was teasing Pee Doodle and bet him $5.00 that he wouldn't sneak up and bite the good looking gal on her posterior the next time she came in to gas up her vehicle. Pee Doodle took the bet after much encouragement from Larry Cooper, Dump and Runt, and the rest of the spit and whittle club. So the bet was on and sure enough it wasn't long before the good looking gal in tight shorts showed up at the station.

With the urging of Colonel Foster and the rest of the group, Pee Doodle got down on his hands and knees and crawled around to the driver's side and when she opened the door to get out he got into position for the posterior bit, but she spotted him at the last second and gave him a good swift kick to the side of the head which knocked poor Pee Doodle out cold flat on the driveway. Needless to say, the lady was not happy and got back into her vehicle and roared out of there. Everybody was laughing so hard that they forgot to tend to poor Pee Doodle who was lying in a goofy state out on the driveway. This story became legend around Bells, and I bet some of the good ole boys hanging out in Bells today could probably still tell you about the day Pee Doodle tried to bite the ole gal from the Oklahoma beer joint on the fanny. Larry Cooper doesn't remember if Colonel Foster paid off on the bet to Pee Doodle but he should have for the effort.

While Larry Cooper was working at the station an ole bootlegger from Oklahoma used to bring his vehicle into the station bay, and Dump and Runt would put it up on the rack for repairs. When someone would come in wanting some moonshine, they would lower the vehicle, pour the moonshine, complete the transaction with the customer, and then raise the vehicle back up on the grease rack to hide the brew. Larry didn't realize what they were doing until later, but one day he tasted the moonshine out of a jar and it was smoking and about knocked him down like a kick from a mule. Speaking of mules, an ole boy named Williams, who was tongue tied, used to come into the station with his father who had an old Ford pick-up. The guys would ask him about his two mules who he used to pull an old side cycle mower. They called em' jackrabbits, and this would really make him mad. One day a state trooper was at the station kidding Williams calling his mules jackrabbits. The tongue tied boy said "Don't call em' jackrabbits, they're mules." The officer persisted with the kidding, and Williams got so mad that he actually took a swing at him, missing but catching him on the head with a backswing which knocked the officer out cold on the floor of the station. "I told him not to call my mules jackrabbits." Everybody in the station was so startled that an unusual silence pervaded the room. Then a little nervous laughter started as they picked the officer up on his feet. He dusted himself off, put on his hat, got in his vehicle and left. The officer never said anything more to Williams and no charges were ever filed for striking the officer. Nobody kidded Williams much after that about his mules. Larry also remembers that one of the guys at the station had a pet skunk that had been de fumed which he brought to the station. Sometimes when good looking women would pull up at the station wearing skirts, an attendant would start to clean her windshield while the guy with the pet skunk would put the skunk up to the driver's side window and say "Do you want to see my pet skunk." You can imagine the reaction of the unsuspecting driver and the observations made by the attendants cleaning the windshield. Larry Cooper laughs as he remembers these escapades at the station. It was a great time for a kid growing up in the 40's and 50's in rural America.

Larry related one final story about his uncle, Lynn Cooper, who was quite a character in his time. Lynn was the older brother of Larry's dad, Lewis, and was kind of a jack of all trades. One day he was doing some painting high up on a ladder to the eaves of a two story house when the ladder slipped and he rode it to the ground striking his head and being covered with white paint. Lynn was taken unconscious to the doctor's office and laid out on an examination table. His paint soaked clothes were removed, and he was covered in a white gown. Finally, when he began to come back into consciousness, draped in white, laying in a sterile examination room with white walls and furnishings, he thought he was dead. "Where am I? Am I dead? Is this a morgue? Am I in heaven? Are you angels? What am I doing dressed in white? Why am I so pale and white all over?" Lynn really got worked up. Finally, the nurse and doctor were able to convince Lynn that he was very much alive and that he had suffered a nasty fall. You can only imagine the kidding poor Lynn would undergo in and around Ely as the story made the rounds. Larry remembers his dad, Lewis, getting a big laugh ever time he would tell the story. But, he had one that even topped this one. It seems that Lynn purchased a brand new Model T Ford when he returned from fighting in France after World War 1. Lynn, a single man, lived on the farm with his dad, Mack, and the rest of the family, including Lewis. The farm was located in Fannin County, Texas, about one mile south of Ely. Ely was a small farming community located about four miles east of Whitewright. The farm was known as "Cooper's Pasture," and the Cotton Belt Railroad line ran through the farm. Lynn was very proud of this new contraption but didn't know much about how to maintain it. One thing that he did do was to keep the crankcase full of oil. One day the Model T just wouldn't start. Lynn tried everything to get it started. Nothing worked. Lewis suggested that Lynn get old George Bennett to come over and take a look since he was the reputed expert mechanic on these new machines in and around Ely, and in fact owned a

Model T himself. When George arrived he tried several tricks but nothing worked. He even tried pulling it with mules to get it up to speed for a rolling start but to no avail. Finally, he noticed something very unusual. Oil was leaking out of the exhaust pipe. "Lynn, how often do you change the oil in your T?" Lynn looked a little puzzled and replied, "What so you mean, change the oil? All I do is add oil to the crankcase." George immediately got a big grin on his face and said "Lynn, I think we can solve your problem." They proceeded to drain the oil from the crankcase, and then filled it with just the right amount of new oil. After several efforts, Lynn's Model T started and didn't miss a beat for many years to come. Well, you can imagine how this story spread throughout the county like a wild fire. Between Lewis and George everybody within fifty miles knew about Lynn Cooper and his Model T oil saga. Larry gets a good laugh as he relates this story about his uncle Lynn and his dad, Lewis, and says, "You know those were great times."

XI.
"I FILLED UP IN HELENA"

ONE DAY WHILE CHARLES E. Perry and I were visiting our friend, Everett Riggs, and several other lawyers and staff in the law offices of our new friend and fellow barrister, A. Clifford Edwards of Billings, Montana, he related the following story about a lawyer he knew who had a drinking problem and finally decided to shake it after two traumatic experiences left him not knowing where he was and how he got there. It seems one day the lawyer while on business back east woke up under a seat in the Cincinnati airport not knowing where he was or how he got there. He vowed to quit drinking when he finally got home. But, not long after this incident, he fell off the wagon again while on business in Helena. On his way home he passed out behind the wheel of his car, went off the roadway, rolled over 5 times, and ended up in the bar ditch. The drunken lawyer was awakened by a tapping on the door window and on looking out saw a man in a uniform with a hat with a star on the brim peering through the window at him. The lawyer finally got the window rolled down and the man in the hat asked if he could help him. The groggy lawyer said "No. I filled up in Helena." He had mistaken the person for a gas attendant at a Texaco station wearing the hat with the big, bright Texaco star on the brim. Needless to say, he was taken to county jail to sleep it off. When he awakened, he saw a drunk who he knew on the cot across the cell from him. The lawyer started to holler down the hall that they couldn't hold an important lawyer like him in a jail cell with this drunk. Then the drunk turned to the lawyer and said, "Your not very important or very smart if you can't figure out how to get out of here. Why, you're just an ole drunk like me." The lawyer looked at the drunk, then took a good hard look at himself and finally decided once and for all that enough was enough and so he quit and has been sober to this very day. Cliff says that the moral to this story is not to mix gasoline and beer or you might end up in the drunk tank just like his lawyer buddy.

XII.
"PITCHIN AT THE LINE FOR THE ROCK"

AT THE CORNER OF CALIFORNIA Street and Cedar St. on U.S. Highway 82, the Lubbock Highway, in Seymour, Texas, and about two blocks from my home on Washington St. stands an old Phillips 66 station built by H. F. Harmel. The oil company, Phillips 66 is named after the famous Route 66 which traversed mid America to California on what was probably the most famous highway and route of travel in America during the 20th Century. This station was operated by Bill Garner and later by Hubert Thornhill. Just east of this station stands probably Seymour's best known and most frequented establishment, The Rock Inn Café, which is an oasis to hungry travelers and especially to the thousands of Texas Tech University students passing through to and from school. The original cafe consisted of a rock building about 20 feet square with one hand operated gas pump in front. According to my resident historian and friend, Jack Jones, Homer Barham bought the west half of the block where the Rock Inn is located. There was a frame house owned by Siddens family on the SW corner of the tract where LaVoy Ball now lives. Homer built the Rock Inn station facing California Street and operated it. Then he started selling hamburgers and put 6 stools and a counter in the building. That is the part of the cafe in the northwest corner of the building at the present time. I can remember as a very small boy going in, sitting at the counter, and ordering a hamburger from Mrs. Jeter, who was one of the waitresses in the late 40's and early 50's. I think the Rock has its origins after World War II when G. I. 's were returning from the war looking for opportunities in business. Well, Homer, certainly found his because the Rock became a very successful enterprise with an excellent location. The business was later sold to the Tidwell brothers who ran it for many years, and one of the brothers even lived in the old Siddens house at the back of the property. Naturally, the Phillips 66 station next door greatly benefited from the Rock Inn traffic.

As a kid, I used to hang out some at this station especially in the back where I was introduced to a fascinating game. One day in our early teens, John Arthur Underwood said lets go over and see what's going on at the Phillips station. We walked over and several guys were in the back including among others, if I remember correctly, Charles Garner, Lynn Thornhill, and Buzzy Jackson. They were playing a game of chance called "pitchin at the line." I had never played this game before but had probably seen it before then. But this day, John Arthur and I jumped in. The object of this game was for the contestants to back off about 20 feet from a line in the concrete floor running perpendicular to where they were standing. Each contestant would throw a coin at the line, usually quarters, and the contestant with the coin closest to the line at the end of each round picked up all of the quarters. This could lead to a quite spirited contest especially during the lunch hour when many players stopped off before going into the Rock Inn to try and win their lunch money. The rules were very loose and anyone could enter the game at any time. Naturally, in the spirit of the game, it didn't look good if a player played only long enough to win a round. The unspoken law of the game was that you played long enough to give the other players a chance to win back your take of quarters. An acceptable number of rounds were usually 10 to 20 rounds of play, or when ever you ran out of money, which ever event occurred first. There were many techniques developed by players in tossing the coin. Some of these were the roller, the high arch, the flip, the saucer, the angle, etc. A player employing the roller technique would let the coin go close to the floor on its edge with just enough velocity and speed to get near the line. The high arch saw the player softly loft the coin in a high arch to come down near the line. The flip employed a back flipping motion of the coin with the thumb hoping for a back spinning motion of the coin as it landed near the line. The saucer technique uses the index finger and thumb to spin the coin in a circular motion toward the target line hoping for a soft landing with little bounce. My friends and I had a lot of fun growing up playing this game and occasionally I made enough for a "chicken fry" at the Rock. What a treat.

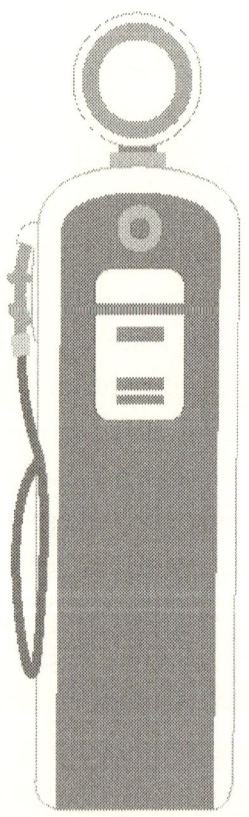

XIII.
"BILL BOYD AND BAYLOR"

WHEN I GOT TO BAYLOR University as a freshman in the fall of 1965 I lived in Penland dormitory and had no wheels as my parents had determined that it wouldn't be wise for me to drive my ole 54' Mercury the some 250 miles from Seymour to Waco. Therefore, most of my prowling around during my freshman year was done in and around campus. One of the places I used to hang out was the Roger Eden's Baylor Drug Store at the corner of 5th and Speight on the south side of the campus next door to the Tidwell Bible Building where all freshmen enrolled in Religion 101 and 102. My favorite recitation on entering its hallowed halls was "Tidwell Tower Give Us Power." I spent many an hour in that building as a freshman under the tutelage of Cecil Sampson, my beloved professor of religion who always began class with a word of prayer. Professor Sampson was a good, gentle man and I respected and learned a lot from him. After class I would saunter over to Baylor Drug for a soda and some pinball and sometimes would wonder on down a half block south on 5th Street to my favorite gas station in all of Waco, Bill Boyd's Texaco. Bill had lived around the Baylor campus all of his life and during his student days had been one of the early bear mascot trainers. My dad knew Bill when he was in law school at Baylor in the mid 30's and would always stop by and say hello to him when visiting me on campus and to buy some gas. Bill was a unique individual. He probably knew more Baylor history than any person alive at the time including Abner McCall, the then President of Baylor and a classmate of my dad. If I remember correctly, Bill's mother ran a boarding house just off campus and so even as a little kid he was around Baylor students. He always had the stub of a cigar in the corner of his mouth as he went about his business around the station. His station was a necessary stop for all visiting alumni to get the latest news on campus. Baylor got its first live bear mascot in 1917 whose name was Ted but sometimes called Bruin. When Bill came along as a student in the 30's the mascot was called Judge, and he took special care of this big black bear. When he died a taxidermist prepared him, and Judge was put on display in the Student Union Building where he remained for several years. Bill would feed Judge Dr. Peppers at the football games, and Judge loved to hold the bottle with his paws and lap up the sweet beverage. Dr. Pepper originated in Waco and naturally the company loved the publicity. Bill hauled that bear all over the country to ball games, and the bear was always the hit of the party. I loved to visit with Bill and let him relive some his stories about Baylor and the bears. He was one of a kind. A living legend of Baylor history you might say. Bill Boyd's station was an institution, and many a Baylor student has fond memories of going there. In reviewing this book, Jack Jones reminded me that the Tidwell Bible Building was named for Dr. J. B. Tidwell and related the following story to me. As you mentioned in a recent conversation, there is a J. B. Tidwell building on Baylor's campus. During my last term in Baylor, which was the spring of 1943, I had an elective. I wanted to take a course under Dr. J. B. Tidwell, so I took "The Life of Christ and the Four Gospels." If I remember correctly, Dr. Tidwell taught at Decatur College when your grandfather was a student there. Tidwell was 83 years old when I took this course. He didn't follow much of a teaching pattern and often just talked about anything someone in the class suggested. One day various members of the class were asking questions. He had seated us in alphabetical order. A lovely sophomore girl, Jacquelyn "Jackie" Keitt, of Hubbard, Texas, was sitting by me. She kept waving her hand and finally Dr. Tidwell pointed his finger at her and said, "My dear, what is your question?" Jackie said, "Well, Dr. Tidwell, when we get to Heaven, will a man recognize his wife and will the wife recognize her husband?" Tidwell replied, "My dear, I hope not because I would have five of them after me."

Jack further said that a few days after your grandmother died, Bro. Balch got a letter from Dr. Tidwell which in part said, "Now Bob, I know that your congregation loves you and would do anything for you. I would suggest that you ask them for about a six week leave and you come to Waco and stay with me. Every preacher needs a wife. If you will come here, I will introduce you to five or six widows and you can pick one out and possibly acquire a new wife." Bro. Balch showed that letter to my mother and Mrs. J. M. Edwards. They could hardly believe that Tidwell would have done such a thing. It seems that Dr. Tidwell had taught my grandfather when he was a student at Decatur College and/or Baylor University. Decatur College was a Baptist school in Decatur, Texas, and was purportedly the oldest junior college anywhere. My grandfather, James Robert Balch, then attended Baylor University where he graduated in 1910, before becoming a Baptist minister and marrying my grandmother, Bertha Holt.

XIV.
"MY DOG SPARKY"

HE WAS MY SECOND DOG as a boy. He was a reddish blond Cocker Spaniel who was my friend throughout my childhood and teenage years. His name was Sparky, and he survived for over fifteen years even after being run over by cars on at least two occasions and being stolen only to find his way back home. He was my best friend and his love was unconditional. We were inseparable. Every where I went Sparky would follow. He was an outside dog who had the run of the town which had no leash law on the books in the 50's and 60's. Everybody in Seymour knew Sparky and that he lived at the Balch house on North Washington Street. Sparky loved people and would approach anyone with that tail wagging and that unforgettable cocker face asking for a pat of acceptance. One of his favorite hangouts was the Clinton Badgwell Humble station at the southeast corner of Oak and California streets. This location was a part of the original premises of the Wichita Valley Railroad Depot. The station was built by Roy Butler and operated by Mr. Badgwell for many years. Clinton's father-in-law, Phylander Greenleaf Allen, operated an Ozark station at the corner of Reiman and Washington Streets just south of the Courthouse on the southwest corner of the square. Clinton learned the trade working for his wife, Pauline's father. He later took over the Humble station. This location was bordered on the west by the railroad tracks, and Sparky loved to watch the trains go by. He would let out a long painful howl when the trains blew their whistles at this intersection because the noise hurt his ears. Sparky never chased the train but would just sit and face it at about a distance of twenty feet. It was very entertaining to watch him, and I know that the guys at the station got a big kick out of watching ole Sparky serenade the trains as they passed by heading south to Abilene. In my mind's eye and ear I can see and hear him just now as I write this tribute. No boy could have had a better dog. When Sparky was not serenading the trains he would often sit at the station and watch the cars and people within come and go. He got many a pat and sometimes even some candy from the patrons. Clinton didn't seem to mind having Sparky around because he never barked at the customers. On Saturdays during the fall the Humble Southwest Conference football game of the week with Kern Tipps would be playing on the radio, and Sparky and I loved to hang out and listen to the game. I would sit on a stack of empty wooden soda pop racks and Sparky would lie down by me in the shade and take a nap. As I recall, Mr. Badgwell had a black collie dog that would come to the station with him, and the collie and Sparky got along well.

Sparky loved to follow me to school first to elementary, just three blocks from my house on Washington Street, then to junior high and high school just five blocks from my house. He would lie down on the school grounds and wait for me to reappear. Sometimes I would tell Sparky to go home and he would sadly obey.

Sparky loved to shag baseballs. He was the best at sniffing out a lost ball. He would follow the gang to Sticker Stadium where many a pick up game was played. He would take his position behind the catcher or in the outfield if I took one of these positions. Sparky would go for any ball if you gave the command "get the ball Sparky, get the ball." With a little coaching he would bring it back to you and wait for the next play. The only problem I had with Sparky was if I didn't put up the baseballs, he would bury them one by one somewhere in the yard. I lost many a good ball because of my lack of diligence in hiding the balls from him in the house. He was known all over town as a good ball shagger. I will never forget that look on his face with a baseball in his mouth looking my way to see if it was his or if my command to bring me the ball was forthcoming.

As he got older and his arthritis got worse, Sparky couldn't follow me any more. I put him in the house during those cold winter nights. Finally, during the spring one year Sparky left his home on Washington Street for the last time. I don't know what happened to him, but he probably wanted to spare me from finding him. It broke my heart, and I never wanted another dog. I loved that dog so much. I still miss him. It has been over forty years now since Sparky left home. My family and I have had many dogs over the years and in fact have three today. Within a month after we married, Debbie and I bought a cocker spaniel which we had for many years. I have loved all of my dogs, but there will never be another Sparky.

XV.
"THE STATION ON RIVER STREET"

A NEW CHEVRON WAS BUILT on the Lubbock Highway at the southwest corner of California and River streets in Seymour in the early 60's by Bill Thornhill, and Roy Morris became its first operator when I was in high school. Roy had previously operated the station across the street west of the First Baptist Church on the southwest corner of Washington and Nevada streets which had been built by Mrs. N. P. Mitchell in 1936. Roy was successful at this location before moving on to the new Chevron station on the Lubbock highway. His son and my friend, James Roy Morris, worked at the new station. Naturally, being located on River Street not far from the Brazos River, it became a good meeting spot for guys going to and from the river. James Roy, Terry Stanford, John Arthur Underwood, Ed Covington, Danny Cockroft, myself, Ronnie Bowman, who worked at the station, and others all congregated here and planned trapping, fishing, and hunting expeditions to the river, Chapman's Lake, Lake Kemp, various farm tanks and other locations. We set traps, placed trot lines, built hunting blinds and set out decoys at various times of the year. Duck and geese were good hunts as well as quail and dove in season. Crappie, bass and catfish were always a good catch as well as the occasional snapping or soft shell turtle, and the largest one I ever saw was brought to Roy's station in a five gallon bucket. Frog hunting with gigs and 22's was a good sport in the hot summer evenings. There is no doubt that more wild game was displayed at Roy's station than anywhere else in town. Even the occasional deer, wild turkey, or feral hog would show up to be seen and the story of the kill told to admiring customers and the guys. Ed Covington related a story to me about a particular goose hunting trip in James Roy's 1940 Green Buick which he became the proud owner of during his freshman year in high school in 1962. It seems that Ed, James Roy and Terry Stanford took the green goose as it was affectionately known on a hunting trip to Gilliland in search of the great Canadian goose. They were very successful in the hunt and pitched all the geese in back and raced back to Seymour in hopes of avoiding the game warden. On reaching Seymour, James Roy pulled into the station and right into the bay for oil changes. They hollered at everybody at the station to come and see the fruits of their big hunt. When they opened the back end of the big Buick dead geese were everywhere and sitting on top was a not so dead goose who was very aggravated at being trapped in the back of the big Buick. He honked and began flapping his wings sending feathers everywhere and nearly knocked the surprised hunters to the ground as he flew out of the station across the Lubbock highway and over the house across the highway heading west. Ed said it was quite a sight and believes that Roy Morris and J.H. Coltharp witnessed this funny episode along with the tired hunters. Well, I have many a fond memory of that ole station on River Street and appreciate Roy and his son, James Roy, letting us hang out there during our high school days.

XVI.
"A FATHER AND SON TEAM"

IN LATE 50'S FRANK KECK, the Texaco consignee in Seymour, built a new Texaco service station at the southwest corner of California and Foley Streets just one block north of the old Seymour High School. The house on the premises which had been the home of the Tom George family and Tom's bachelor brother-in-law, Parks McLarty, was moved by the Holman family to the southeast part of town where it is occupied to this date. The first operator of the new station was a fellow from Benjamin who it is alleged loved the spirits more than the work so he didn't last long. Then came Charles H. Sessions, who had operated the Mobil station at the southwest corner of Washington and Oregon streets where the fire station now stands, and who operated this Texaco station until his death with the help of his son, Charles Thomas Sessions, who continues to occupy the premises to this day. Although he no longer sells gasoline, Charles Thomas does auto inspections and washes and services vehicles. He is also a Justice of the Peace for Baylor County. This family has operated this station for nearly 50 years at this location. I went to high school with Charles Thomas who was a grade ahead of me, and he married my classmate and friend, Sandra Henshaw. As you can imagine, being only one block from the high school, there was always something going on and people hanging out. This was a favorite station for Texas Tech students and many a lovely coed was observed and flirted with during her stop at the big bright Texaco star. I liked to pull up in my 54 Mercury, put in a couple of bucks worth of gas and then pull over to the side and watch the traffic. I parked on the street headed south and would walk the half block or so to school. It was a perfect vantage point. Mud Dickson's little store was only a half block to the east, and I would often walk over there for lunch and a few words of wisdom from Mud. He was quite a character wearing his French beret and expounding behind the counter of his little grocery store. Life was simple and times were good in the era after WWII. People of Mud's and Charles H.'s generation seemed to appreciate what they had and certainly weren't afraid of a little hard work. I learned a lot watching these guys go about their daily routines. They always had time for a smile and some conversation with their customers. We could use a little more of this today in this fast paced world we live in. I guess you could sum this up by saying, "take time to smell the roses."

XVII.
"THE COURTHOUSE SQUARE"

As I was growing up in the 50's, the center of activity in Seymour took place around the courthouse square where an imposing multi-story stone structure built in the 1880's served as the seat of county government. Later, in the early 60's, my dad moved his law office to a small building facing the courthouse on the south side of the square on Reiman Street. I spent many an hour in his office and going back and forth from the courthouse. The old jail sat on the southeast corner of the courthouse square. Prisoners would see my dad walking back and forth to his office and would often yell loudly, "Judson come get me out." My dad always got a good laugh and sometimes would go over and post bond for his clients. I learned early on that a lawyer was in high demand when someone was in trouble with the law or was being sued in civil court. There are a lot of lawyer jokes out there and many folks think lawyers are less than honest, but your know, the truth is that lawyers are advocates for their client's position, and when you need one, he or she is the greatest, most trustworthy guy or gal in town. Lawyers protect people's liberties and try to protect the due process of law rights of the citizenry. It will be a sad day in this country if a lawyer can't plead his or her client's case before a jury of peers without interference from the government or third party interests. All Americans must fight to protect the jury system in this country. My dad always felt strongly about these issues and so do I in the 21st century. Well let me get off my soapbox and talk about the courthouse square of the 50's and 60's. Free enterprise was everywhere around the courthouse square. At the southeast corner of Washington and Reiman, just west of my dad's law office stood an Ozark fillin' station operated originally by Phylander Greenleaf Allen. Most of the time there was a garage in the rear. It has always been a gathering place to discuss politics and local events. Today, it's no longer a station and known as T.J.'s place. At the northwest corner of Washington and Reiman on the west side of the courthouse square stood a Mobil station facing diagonally southeast. It was operated by Luther and Otis Thomas. After World War II this structure was torn down and replaced by the present structure. It was operated by Henry Gray Briggs and Mud Dickson. Mud also operated a taxi service out of this place. Later, Charles Sessions, and finally Denver Carlyle was the last operator before it was abandoned. I think Denver also operated a radiator repair shop out of this place. I knew his son, Kenny, who worked with his dad and also worked for Elmo Hooser at the local theater and drive-in. Moving on around the courthouse square, on the southwest corner of Washington and McLain stood the old Harvey and later the Brazos Hotel. On the street Roy Quisenberry, Sr. had a gas station which I think sat diagonally at the corner with a large overhang for the customers to drive under for service. After World War II, Carl and Roy, Jr. operated the station. Finally, Roy, Jr. remodeled it into office space. David Hajek and Chad Williams are lawyers who have occupied the premises. Graham Quisenberry, grandson of Roy Sr. and son of Roy Jr., advises me that this was a Mobil station with a Goodyear Tire franchise, also. He said that they recapped tires during the war and for sometime after. His grandfather also built the rock station that formerly sat on the Abilene highway at the Throckmorton highway turn, as well as a station that was located at the site of the Martin Motors Chrysler dealership. According to Graham, his grandfather was also associated with Magnolia Oil, a predecessor of Mobil, as well as a Texaco distributorship. Graham has a picture of his dad on a parade float bearing the Texaco emblem from the 20's. He says that there are a couple of Magnolia signs at his parents' home in Seymour, and he has an old Badger Tire sign at his house. Graham is a lawyer and now a judge in Weatherford, Parker County, Texas.

At the southwest corner of Washington and Reiman a gas station was established and operated by Mr. Allen who had the Ozark station across the street to the east. In about 1946, Woody Montgomery rented a stall behind the station and started trading tractors. Jack Jones loaned Woody $300.00 to buy a tractor. That night Woody painted it red and sold it the next day for $500.00. That was his start, and Woody built his business into one of the world's largest used tractor and farm equipment auction businesses right in Seymour, and it is still in business today at a location on the Wichita Falls, Highway 82/277. I believe that later a Firestone franchise was operated out of this building by Joe Cuba and George Holub, and finally a parts supply house last run by Dickie Thurmond before the structure burned.

As a kid I can remember hanging around all of these stations. There was always a domino game going at the Ozark. The Carlyle station was next door to Clarence Wilbanks' City Market. His slogan was "Cut em' with a fork." He was a great butcher and provided quality meats. He also extended credit to his customers. Up the block, the Quisenberry station was next to the Club Café, which was a mighty fine eating establishment run by Slim Temple. Nearby, Mary Feemster and her brother, Lonnie Cox, operated the Liberty Café. I could walk to any of these places from my dad's office and sometimes he would go with me. Sometimes I would sneak off and climb to the dome of the old courthouse to pester the pigeons roosting up there and to look out over the city of Seymour and think to myself how lucky I was to be growing up in this small town in the 50's. The ole courthouse is gone now, having given way to a modern single story structure which is attractive and efficient, but I somehow still long to see that old courthouse of my youth, which has passed into the annals of history taking with it many fond memories and events. I have a picture plate of that old courthouse in my law office and below the picture it reads Baylor County Courthouse, Seymour, Texas 1884-1967. When I look at it I think about my dad and all the years he spent practicing law there. Those are great memories.

XVIII.
"HARD WORK PAYS OFF"

IN THE 60's TWO BROTHERS, Clayton and Mike Brasher, bought a gas station from Charlie Hutt financed by Jack Jones. Located at 1001 N. Main on the west side of Highway 82/277, the Brasher brothers went to work at building their business. I have known these boys for most of their lives, and their dad and mom were in the mattress building business, where they learned their work ethics. These brothers built a thriving business which is still going strong into the 21st century. They have since built a restaurant on the site and have also purchased several farms. If you want to learn a lesson in how hard work pays off, the Brasher brothers are a good example to study.

XIX.
"THE GIN"

RECENTLY, I HAD A GOOD visit with Cindy, Craig, and Melody McNeill and their mother, Marguerite. Their family ran the McNeill Gin located just north of the Brasher Brothers station at 1100 N. Main on the East side of Highway 82/277. A gas station was operated in connection with the gin. Their granddad and father-in-law, A. J. McNeill, and their father and husband, Edwin McNeill, ran this station as a retailer for R. L. Moore. This location is now a part of the Seymour Culvert Complex. The gin was a hub of activity during the cotton harvest season. I loved to go out there and watch the process from the raw cotton at intake until a nice clean 500 lb. bale of cotton rolled off the line and into the storage area. Warehouse receipts were issued and cotton buyers began the process of marketing the cotton. Warehouse fires were a constant threat during ginning season and the fine white lint covered the area. We kids knew when the fire alarm sounded that there was a good chance it would be in response to a fire at the gin so off we would go on our bikes to view the excitement. The McNeill kids grew up on Washington Street just 2 doors north of my house. We can relive many adventures, ball games and events that took place in the neighborhood. I echo what they said to me at our recent visit, that they wouldn't take anything for those experiences growing up in that neighborhood in Seymour, and, you know something, neither would I looking back over all the fun times we had together along with the other neighborhood kids.

XX.
"EARL AND FLOYD'S PLACE"

AT THE NORTHEAST CORNER OF N. Main and Nevada Streets, Dr. R. K. Lowery built a station. Earl Chandler operated the Conoco station for several years. Earl was a great guy. I rode my bike to his station on many a summer's day to put air in my tires on my way to the city park and swimming pool. Taking Nevada east would take you to Fair Park Hill, Anna's Damn, and the City Park with its huge trees along the creek and a wonderful old swimming pool that I loved. Earl always took time to greet me and have some conversation. He worked hard and had a lot of steady customers including my family. Across the street west from Earl's place, Floyd Bench operated a Gulf station. Floyd was quite a character. His station was across the street north of the BK Electric Coop and the First Baptist Church parking lot. Sometimes, I would pull thru Floyd's station for a soda pop and to get some local news before heading across to the FBC parking lot for Chapel Choir practice. I've got some good memories of those guys and their stations. Floyd's station is gone, and a vacant lot stands in its place today. Earl's station is gone, and the County bought the property from the Lowery family and built offices on the site.

XXI.
"JACK JONES
REMEMBRANCES"

I asked one of the resident historians of Seymour and Baylor County for most of the 20th century and my friend, Jack Jones, to come up with his list of fillin' stations in Seymour. He graciously provided me a list of some 53 stations with a narrative about most of them. I have drawn from this list and these narratives in this writing and so thought it would be appropriate to print it here in its entirety. Naturally, I asked Jack's permission to do so. It is quite entertaining, done in fun, and hopefully no one will take offense to any of these stories. So, Jack these are your remembrances:

FILLIN' STATIONS IN SEYMOUR

1. SW Corner of California and River St--operated by Simon Benge, Billy Benge, Roy Morris and Whit Powell. Think was a FINA station. This was the location of the Arden house back in the 1920s. Later was occupied by Jack St. Clair and Mrs. W. T. Britton. The house has been moved and is now on the north part of Starlight Drive. This station has been closed for several years.

2. NW Corner of California and Arkansas St.—A COSDEN (John Underwood says it was a FINA)--station—built by a dealer from Ft. Worth. This location was the home of J. T. White. After Mr. White died, the house was moved by R. J. Laney to a location in the extreme NE part of Seymour. The abandoned station has been bought by Wayland Jones. He and his wife store stuff there.

3. SW Corner of California and Foley St.—TEXACO station built by Frank Keck. First operator was a guy from Benjamin who drank a lot and didn't do too good. Then Charles H. Sessions took over and operated until he died, then Charles T. Sessions. This was the location of the home of the Tom George family and Tom's bachelor brother in law, Parks McLarty. The house was moved to the SE part of town by either Dave or Lynn Holman and is still on the east side of the Old Folks Housing. Charles T. Station still washes a few cars there and does auto inspections.

4. NE Corner of California and Foley St.—This location was vacant because of flooding until the storm sewer system was built. It was Old Man W. E. England's cow lot. Then Bernie Neatherly, Mrs. England's son in law built a station there and operated it for Bell Oil and Gas Co. Later Jim Lovelace bought the place and put an Allsup's Store there. England had another son in law, Carroll Duke who was president of a bank in Iowa Park.

He said that Carroll Duke was his son in law and Bernie was the Old Lady's. It is now occupied by Santa Rosa Coop Telephone Co.

5. SE Corner of California and Foley St.—This place was vacant because of flooding until the storm sewer was built. Then Ethel Tom "Bud" Bledsoe and his brother in law named Overstreet put a restaurant there. Later Art Mitchell operated the restaurant. Then a Mobil station was built on the location. Maybe Kotulek, Woody Montgomery's son in law had something to do with it. Then it was operated by J. T. Duncan. This station was never profitable. Later Lewis Wade Caussey put his drive-in there. The place now vacant.

6. NE Corner of California and Cedar St.—A man named Thomas had a large house at this location. It was torn down or moved and a Bell Oil and Gas Co. station was built there. Either before or after the station, Bird Franklin had a small grocery store at this place. Tom Sessions also operated the store either before or after Franklin. Now Randy Coltharp has a garage there.

7. SE Corner of California and Cedar St.—H. F. Harmel built a Phillips 66 Station on this location it was operated by Bill Garner and later by Hubert Thornhill. Phillips 66 was named after Highway 66. The place is now owned by Ralph Malone's brother, James.

8. Just east of the Phillips 66 Station was the original Rock Inn Station. It consisted of a rock building about 20 ft. square with one hand operated gas pump in front. Homer Barham bought the west half of the block where the Rock Inn is located. There was a frame house owned by the Siddens family on the SW corner where Lavoy Ball lives. Homer built the Rock Inn Station and operated it. Then he started selling hamburgers and put about 6 stools and a counter in the building. That is the part of the café in the northwest corner of the building at the present time. (See Museum News history of the Rock Inn.)

9. NW Corner of California and Oak St.—A Texaco station was built there. It was operated by Denver Carlyle, Nolan Davis and Jimmy Martin. It is now abandoned. (John Underwood says that this was a Gulf station operated by J. W. Holmes and later converted to a Texaco.)

10. SE Corner of California and Oak St.—This is the location of the Humble station which was built by Roy Butler and operated for many years by Clinton Badgwell. (John Underwood says after Badgwell then by Morris Gambrill, who was Butch Naylor's father-in-law, until a tire blew off the rim and injured him. Then by a one eyed guy by the name of Earl Williams.) Later by a one eyed guy named Williams. This location was a part of the original premises of the Wichita Valley Railroad Depot. It is now an auto repair garage.

11. NW Corner of California and Washington St.—
   There was a large house at this location years ago.
   After something happened to the house a Texaco
   station was built on the corner. It was operated by
   Frank Keck's brother, Walter. Later, Ray Jaco had
   a hamburger joint in a trailer. Then Adolph Wirz
   built Art Mitchell a restaurant there. Adolph told me
   what he was going to do. I asked him what kind of
   building he was going to build. He said a concrete
   block building about like the Maverick is now. I said,
   "Adolph, why don't you go to Wichita and spend a
   few dollars and get an architect to design something
   half way decent?" After a couple of cups of coffee he
   reluctantly took my advice. In a day or two he came
   in with the plans and was tickled to death with the
   way the front of the building was designed. I studied
   the plans. The only rest rooms in the building were in
   the front of the place between the two dining areas. I
   said, "Adolph this all looks great with one exception.
   You need to put another crapper in the back of the
   building. If you don't, then when all the nice folks
   in town are dining there, a cook or dishwasher with
   a filthy apron on and a cigarette hanging out his
   mouth will parade through the dining room to go to
   the pot." After another argument, he agreed to turn
   loose a few more dollars and put in the extra crapper.
   The cafe was operated for several years by Art and
   then sold a couple of times. (John Underwood says
   that Dick and Fred Wirz donated the building to the
   City. The City owns the property now and uses it for
   Police Headquarters.)

12. SW Corner of California and Washington St.—
    Panhandle Petroleum Co. built a station that
    faced the intersection diagonally. This location
    was also the distribution location for Panhandle.
    W. A. "Bun" Melear was the Panhandle agent and
    operator of the station. I think that later Robert
    Crowell may have operated the station. Then it was
    torn down and a new brick station was built. This
    is now the location of James Cooper's car lot. John
    Orsak worked for Bun. I can see him now, putting
    gasoline into a tank truck while puffing on a cigar. I
    waited and waited for an explosion, but it never did
    occur.

13. SE Corner of California and Washington St.—The
    Webb family had a large frame home on this corner.
    Mr. Webb built a small fillin' station on the corner
    with the pumps facing Washington St. I think that
    it was after he and Mrs. Webb passed on that his
    daughter, LaVerne and husband, A. J. Ballerstedt
    built the two story building and two houses that
    occupy the premises at this time. Bill Culver now
    owns the property.

14. NW Corner of California and Main St.—This was
    the location of the J. T. Reeves service station. It was
    a small frame building with hand operated pumps.
    It is now the Dairy Queen location.

15. NE Corner of California and Main St.—This is now
    the location of Allsups. I sold the south 50 ft. of this

place to Jim Lovelace when he moved to Seymour. I told him at the time that I considered this the primary corner between Ft. Worth and Lubbock. I still think that it is. As people died off—Charlie Richmond, Turner Shaver, Jim Cooper and Tom Bledsoe—Jim was able to buy additional property until he has the large location where he built the Allsup store.

16. SW Corner of California and Main. This location has had a station for many years. The original one faced East and was a Texaco Station. A few years ago, that one was destroyed and replaced with the modern one operated by Rick Meaders. It is probably one of the most profitable ones in town since it is on the prime corner.

17. NE Corner of Washington and Nevada. This is across the street north of the Baptist Church. R. L. Moore was manager of the Waggoner Estate. He bought gasoline from their Electra Refinery for 3 cents a gallon and built fillin' stations around the area. This was one of them. It wasn't there too long, but it was still one of the old stations in town.

18. NW Corner of Washington and Nevada. This was a station made famous by Roy Whiteside. He operated this Texaco station for many years.

19. SW Corner of Washington and Nevada. Mrs. N. P. Mitchell built a Sinclair station at this location in 1936 and leased it to Sinclair for $65.00 per month

for 10 years. After a year or two the operator went broke. About every two years Sinclair would send a representative around to ask her to lower the rent and she would refuse. Then when WWII was over, Roy Morris successfully opened the station and Sinclair had to renew the lease, this time for $100.00 per month. One afternoon Roy and Adolph Wirz were having a drink. Morris Randal drove by and stopped to buy some gas. Roy filled up his tank and asked, "Morris, would you like to have a little drink? Morris answered, "Nope, but I'll have a big one." Roy finally moved out on the Lubbock Highway to the station mentioned in #1 above and after another operator or two, the station was abandoned. I appraised the station for Nick Mitchell and he gave it to the church.

20. SW Corner of Washington and Oregon, Mobil had a station where the fire station is now located. It was operated by Charlie Sessions at one time. Then the city acquired it, tore it down and built the fire station.

21. SE Corner of Washington and Oregon, This station was operated by Hop Parker at one time. A gang used to hang out there and shoot craps. One day John M. and I were riding bicycles south on Washington and a dice rolled under our bicycles. We heard someone cussing. It was Henry Gray Briggs, Gerald Farr or Buck Wallace who had just crapped out.

22. SW Corner of Washington and Pecan. There was a station in the corner of a brick building at this location. Morgan Bowman had a Pontiac dealership behind the station. Later that is where Travis Martin started his Alis Chalmers dealership. Then the station was closed and J. O. Butler put the Ford dealership there. After several other occupancies, the building finally rotted down.

23. SW Corner of Washington and McLain. This was the location of the Harvey (Later the Brazos) Hotel. Roy Quisenberry, Sr. had a station at this location. After the war Carl and Roy Jr. operated the place. Roy Jr. finally remodeled it into the office space now at the location.

24. NW Corner of Washington and Reiman, Mobil originally had a station here facing diagonally southeast. It was operated by Luther and Otis Thomas. After WWII it was torn down and replaced by the present structure. It was operated by Briggs & Dickson—Henry Gray Briggs and Mud Dickson. Mud operated a taxi service out of the place as well. Later Charlie Sessions (John Underwood says it was Albert Patterson and that his wife built a beauty shop behind the station) had the station and then I think Denver Carlyle was the last to operate it before it was abandoned. Billy and Randy Benge operate a garage there now.

25. SE Corner of Washington and Reiman. This was the Ozark fillin' station. It was operated by

Phylander Greenleaf Allen. He was the father of Pauline Badgwell. Clinton Badgwell worked for him. Most of the time there was a garage in the rear of the building. Later it was used for various purposes until now it is T. J. 's place.

26. SW Corner of Washington and Reiman. After operating the Ozark, P. G. Allen moved to this location where there was a sheet iron building. He had a station there. About 1946, Woody Montgomery rented a stall behind the station and started trading tractors. I loaned Woody $300.00 to buy a tractor one afternoon. That night he took it to this stall and painted it red. The next day he sold it for $500.00. That was his start. (John Underwood says that George Holub and Joe Cuba had a Firestone store, and it was a Texaco gas station. Frank Keck owned the building.)

27. SE Corner of Washington and Miller. H. F. Harmel built a station there. Later Arthur Lee "Stinkie" Harris had a machinery dealership there and the place was finally abandoned.

28. NE Corner of Washington and Ingram. This was the location of a large house occupied by the Easley family. They had a small frame fillin' station in the corner of the yard. It was called the Buckhead station. It was finally closed about 1950 and later Claude Cowan bought the place and built his office building. It now houses the Jenkins Insurance Agency.

29. SE Corner of Washington and Ingram. A. J. Cooper built a Gulf station on this corner. It was operated by Osee Holand. It was finally abandoned and the location became a part of the parking lot for the motel next door.

30. NW Corner of Washington and Lincoln. This was always a sort of "independent" station (John Underwood says it was an APCO) until Ron Laney bought it and converted it into a self service type. It still is operated by his estate.

31. At Curve where N. Main turns toward Wichita Falls, Tom Head owned about 8 acres of land in this triangle. His home was just south of where the V. V. Overton house is now. In this "V" corner, Tom had a combination fillin' station, café, honky tonk and motel. After Tom died it finally rotted down and has been cleaned off. (John Underwood says that on the West Side of N. Main before you get to the Curve that the Farmers Coop put in fuel in the late 80's or early 90's. John further states that as you turned north on the Lake Road after the Curve that the Bishops had an Exxon station.) (I just had a good visit with Barbara Welch who is the daughter of Cy and Mildred Bishop. She grew up in Seymour and works at the Hallmark Store in the Mall here in Wichita Falls. John Underwood had reminded me that the Bishops had a station on the lake road just off U. S. Hwy. 82 & 277 northeast of town. I called her to get the details. She said that

Cy and Mildred had moved to Seymour in 1946, and he was the agent for Continental Oil Company. He also ran the Buckhead Station at the northeast corner of Ingram and Washington, the Seymour Service Station across the street south of the old hospital at the Southeast corner of Washington and Oregon, and the Humble Station on the Southwest corner of N. Main and Pecan that later was run by Morris Perkins. According to Barbara, Cy envisioned that 82 & 277 would be made into a four lane highway and so bought the land on the lake road in the late 1950's and opened a store on the premises. The family moved the old Melear house on site and moved there in 1962. The store was an Exxon station with two pumps. The family sold some groceries, bait, gas, soft drinks and ice. Cy developed the ice into a commercial business and sold to other businesses in town as well as supplying his customers. Barbara said a fire destroyed the location in the early '70's but that Cy continued the ice business until his death in 1973. Mildred died in 1991 and all of Barbara's siblings are now deceased, Dorothy in 2001, and Buster and Marilyn in 2005. I remember going to that little store as a kid. Barbara and I decided that Cy was a visionary since that big four lane highway is now under construction, but it turned back to the south before it reached the lake road so maybe its better that he didn't live to see it.)

32. East Side N. Main, North of Highway Barn. This is where there is a firecracker stand at present. Garvin

Jones operated a small frame station at this location. There is a firecracker stand there now. Garvin's daughter, Virginia, married Larry Pfau and was one of the best employees Bunkley and Jones ever had. Her son, Russell, has a PhD from Oklahoma State in Biology and is a professor at John Tarleton. Virginia also has a brother named Leo Jones.

33. East Side N. 1100 Main, McNiell Gin. This station was also a retailer for R. L. Moore. A. J. McNeill operated it in connection with the gin. This location is now a part of the Seymour Culvert complex.

34. West side of N. Main, 1001 Brasher Bros. When Clayton & Mike Brasher were about 18-20 years old, Charlie Hutt asked me to loan them $1,800.00 to buy the fillin' station and the land with it. I reluctantly did and visited them regularly. They worked their butts off. I then brokered a loan for them to build their houses. Betsy helped the wives design the houses. Then I loaned them the money to buy the land where they built their restaurant. After they got out of debt, they started to buy land. They wound up with three or four farms. They have been very successful.

35. East Side N. Main, 1002, operated by A.D. "Slugger" Smith. This was a combination convenience store and fillin' station. It is vacant now. There is a "Yard Sale" on the premises about once a month.

36. NW Corner N. Main and Nevada, Floyd Bench

operated this station for years and years. Floyd sold Gulf products. Later Nolan Davis acquired the property and switched it to Texaco. It has been closed for a long time and the station was destroyed. When Sonic was looking for a location, the man came to me and we drove around town. He selected that as his favorite location. Sonic could not make a deal for the property.

37. NE Corner N. Main and Nevada. The station at this location was built by Dr. R. K. Lowry. Earl Chandler operated a station there for several years. The County eventually bought the place from Lowry's daughter and County offices are there now.

38. SE Corner N. Main and Oregon. Foster H. Bunkley built a station on this corner. He leased it to H. F. Harmel and H. F. hired John Baldwin to run it.

39. NE Corner N. Main and Pecan. This station was probably built by the Craddocks. Ferrell Wright operated it for a number of years. For the last several years Billy Benge has had a repair garage there. It is closed now.

40. SW Corner N. Main and Pecan. Jim Morris' sister built this one for an investment. It was a Sinclair Station. Luther Thomas ran it for a while. Then Virgil Bryan; later Gene Robinson and Charles Lee and at another time, John Finn Robinson and Burnett Crowell, and maybe others. It was finally abandoned. (Bob's footnote-Morris Perkins ran

an Exxon station at this site. According to Ralph Perkins, his nephew, who hung out there as a kid, and whose dad, Ruel, worked their after he retired from the post office, this is where he first heard the term "PWI" used to describe no sale customers who just stopped in for a pee, water, and information.)

41. N. Main, Center Block where Lawrence Bros is— Frank and Walter Keck operated a couple of gas pumps on the sidewalk at this location. It was a rock building. The fire trucks were kept there at one time. Next door south was a paint and paper store operated by a man named Rogers and Sparks Burnett. Next door to that, Tom Killman had a café and bus station. (Bob's footnote—my uncle, Garlin Feemster ran the café and bus station for a period during the early 50's.)

42. N. Main, Center West Side 100 Block just south of Farmers Natl drive in, there was a Kerosene pump. Tom and Bill Craddock had a grocery store on the corner and the Kerosene pump was part of that operation.

43. NE Corner S. Main and Miller. This was the Fina distribution center and a fillin' station operated by Robert Crowell. It change hands later and finally Day Carlin bought it. It is vacant now.

44. SW Corner S. Main and Miller. Sam Styles operated a station and junk store there. It is still Junk but vacant.

45. NE Corner S. Main and Ingram. This was a Gulf station. Jack Richardson operated it for several years. It is now the location of Phillip Campbell's body shop.

46. SE Corner Main and Ingram. This was a convenience store with gas station for many years. It has recently been vacated. (Bob's footnote—I think this is the station where Luke Morgan bought the winning Texas lottery number which made him an instant multimillionaire. It couldn't have happened to a nicer, harder working man. My life long friend, Tom Porter and his wife, Patty, with their partners, Darin Hays and his wife, Melissa, have reopened this Shamrock station and convenience store where I understand they are serving up some great food.)

47. SW Corner S. Main and Ingram. Jim Richeson built a station here for Humble. It went broke and was abandoned. There has been a drive in restaurant on the premises, but it is gone now.

48. NW Corner S. Main and Ingram. This was headquarters for the legendary Jack Roddy. After he died, Jim Lovelace bought the land from the Roddy family and built the Allsup's store.

49. NE Corner Ingram and May. Arthur Jones operated a station at this location in connection with his residence, a small motel. The Pritchard family acquired the property and then it was abandoned.

50. SW Corner of Ingram and East St. I don't know who built this dude. It is on the wrong side of the street in the wrong part of town. I can't remember it ever being open. Travis Warren owns the property now and uses it for a place to loaf. (John Underwood says that it was a Texaco and that Cotton Morris was the operator.)

51. West Lincoln north side across river. W. J. Roddy operated this place. There was a restaurant next door and he ran that as well. I think all of this was converted into a residential premises. (John Underwood says it was a Phillips 66 station and that Alford and George Boone were the operators.)

52. At "Y" on Abilene Hy. Bill Keck operated a station in this rock building. It has since been destroyed and is now the location of David Snyder's steel company.

53. Hawkins hill, north side, Flynt Bibb, R. J. Hayley and O. T. Richeson built this place. I refused to assist them with a loan because it was such an impossible location. It was a fancy place with a restaurant and living quarters. It was on the west side of the road. Anyone coming from the west, east bound, would have had to turn into west bound traffic topping Hawkins hill. This would have been a good way to get killed. Westbound traffic would have just passed through Seymour and past at least a dozen service stations. I checked with the Brasher boys. They

said they would not have the place as a gift. Shortly after they finished the place, Hancock Oil Co. from Houston bought the place and it immediately went broke. It was converted to a crumby residence.

Bob, these are the only fillin' stations I can remember "Off the top of my head."

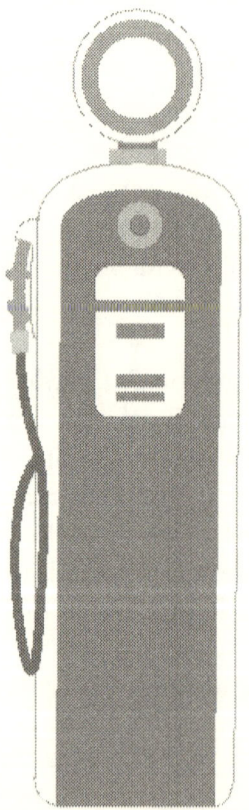

XXII.
"THE MCCLESKEY STATION"

MY COUSINS, JIM, MIKE, CANDACE and Bill Balch, have a fabulous legacy left to them by their granddad and grandmother, Marvin and Mary McCleskey. The couple ran a Texaco station just down the street east from their home on 4th Street in Graham, Texas. Their daughter, Wanda, met my dad's youngest brother, J. B., through a mutual friend and roommate, Billie Gene (Duncan) Young, after World War II while the girls were attending the University of North Texas in Denton, Texas. Romance was in the air and they were soon married after the war. I always used to love to go to Graham as a kid with my cousins to visit the McCleskeys and especially to hang out at their gas station. It was run the old fashion way. Full service was provided including cleaning the windshield, checking the air pressure in the tires, checking the level of the engine oil and water in the radiator, sweeping out the floor board. Customers would go inside for a soda pop and some good conversation with Marvin and his helpers. You could get minor repairs done to your vehicle, get flats fixed, and other maintenance services. Marvin wore the uniform proudly with the green round rimmed hat, the black leather bow tie, and the green shirt and pants. Marvin knew his business and worked hard at the station. This work ethic was passed on to his daughter, Wanda, his son, Allen, and his grandkids, my cousins who I have above named, all of which have doctorate degrees and the three boys are medical doctors. I know Jim and his brothers and sister have many remembrances of their grandparents and the gas station on 4th street in Graham. My Aunt Wanda told me that her dad was always mechanically minded. He loved bicycles and when he came to Graham had one of those big wheel bicycles which he rode around town. Later when Wanda and Allen got bicycles, he got one for himself and put a gasoline engine on it. In the early 30's the McCleskey home at the corner of Virginia and 4th Streets burned due to a problem with a new refrigerator. Marvin was determined to build back and decided to build a station on the corner and a small house behind on Virginia for the family. He got financing from the local Texaco distributor and built it. He went to work driving a truck for the Texaco distributor and got an operator for the station. Later, Marvin became the operator and continued its operation until 1962 when he had a heart attack. Marvin was according to Wanda a "quaint" person. She said he taught all of her kids how to drive in an old standard shift Falcon. Wanda related that he would say. "You've got to get this thing out of grasshopper gear if your going to learn to drive." Her mother, Mary, helped out at the station. The family moved down the street to 924 4th Street and Allen still lives there. When Allen retired from teaching and moved back to Graham in the 80's he took over operations for a while before selling the station. For most of its life it was a Texaco station. At the end it was an Exxon. The ole building still remains there on 4th as a reminder of an era gone by the way.

XXIII.
"THE RACE TO
HAWKINS HILL"

THERE'S ANOTHER STATION THAT HAS not been mentioned that was built on the south side of the Lubbock Hwy. on Hawkins hill just west of Seymour. Ralph Perkins and I were talking about this station but couldn't remember if it was an independent or built by one of the major oil companies. John Underwood says he believes it was originally a Shamrock station. It had a little cafe at the site which was at one time run by Ray Jaco, who was a great short order cook and later had the Bus Burger Restaurant in town. Over all this stood a very tall mock oil derrick which attracted attention to the business. Many an evening my friends and I would get into our vehicles and race to Hawkins Hill. My old 54 Mercury won its share of those races. John Underwood won a few of these races as well. We would go into the cafe for some food and drink, to play a little pin ball and listen to the juke box. This was a fun place, and I always think back to it when I pass the site headed west. In 2005 a new restaurant opened in Wichita Falls called the Pumpjack Diner on Broad Street below the 287 overpass. The establishment has this big ole imitation oil derrick at the site. Its motif is the history of the oil patch in Wichita County and there are many photographs and other memorabilia displayed in the restaurant for the enjoyment of its patrons. I was surprised to learn that the ole oil derrick that towers over the premises was moved in from a site outside of Seymour. Well, you guessed it. The ole oil derrick on Hawkins hill has new life. I get a lot of pleasure every time I pass by the restaurant thinking about those races to Hawkins Hill in the 60's.

XXIV.
"THE CALL"

I sing in the bass section of the choir at my church, and the bass section leader is a fellow named Steve Bernhardt. Steve and I have become friends, and he works at a manufacturing plant with my cousin, Freddie Balch, the son of Lemuel Balch, one of my dad's younger brothers. In his younger days Steve, affectionately nick-named "Teddy Bear" by his friends, worked the night shift at the Taystee Bakery in Wichita Falls, Texas. I can still smell that aroma of freshly baking bread spreading into the air from the bakery. Steve is a great writer in his own right and sends the men of the choir a monthly newsletter with all sorts of enlightenment. The other night after choir we were talking about this book, and he told me a story about one of his funny experiences around a gas station where he hung out in the early morning hours after his shift ended at the bakery. This particular station was located on the old Jacksboro highway and will remain anonymous at the request of Teddy Bear. The night attendant was a little jumpy and always worried about being held up. He liked for Steve to come by and stay a spell because he knew Steve packed heat in his vehicle. One evening the attendant was real excited about an encounter with a local hood who was planning on calling him by telephone with some secret code for him to write down and hold until another hood picked it up so he could get some loot held by a third party. The attendant showed him an old recorder that he was going to use to tape the conversation. When he told Teddy Bear about this it set the wheels in motion.

One night a few days later after Steve got off work, he placed a telephone call to his friend at the station and disguised himself as the hood and gave him a code. "Write these letters and numbers down and hold them for me MC46931. You got that?" The attendant was scrambling around in the background to turn on the recorder and nervously replied, "Yes sir, I sure do." When Steve showed up at the station a little while later the attendant was very excited and waved for him to come over quickly to the recorder. The attendant was so nervous that he could hardly talk. Before he could turn it on Steve began to question him about the call and finally asked if the code was MC46931. Suddenly, the attendant realized that he had been tricked by the Teddy Bear who by now was laughing so hard that he could hardly stand up. Teddy Bear made a quick retreat to his vehicle before his friend could get even by hitting him with whatever might be handy like a tire tool. For several days the Teddy Bear steered clear of the station until his friend had time to cool down. Steve doesn't think that his friend ever got that call from the hood, but he would never forget the call from the Teddy Bear that set this prank in motion.

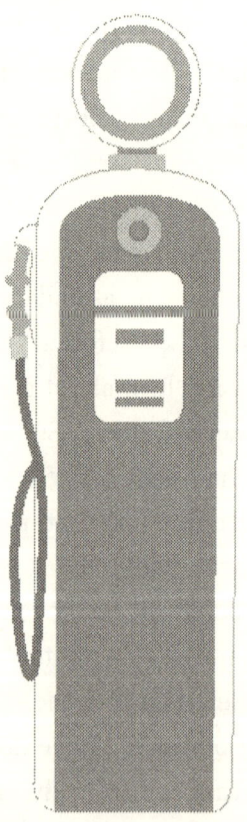

XXV.
"COLD CANDY"

My friend Barbara Kafer is a school teacher who grew up in Clay County, Texas, on a farm 2 miles from Hurnville, a small farming community located 10 miles north of Henrietta, the county seat. Barbara is a good friend of fellow teacher, Janice Vita Thornhill, who I grew up with in Seymour, Texas. Both Barbara and Janice are Midwestern State University graduates and shared an apartment when they began their teaching careers with Janice at Henrietta and Barbara at Burkburnett. In any event, while growing up on the farm in the years following WWII, Barbara's dad, Oscar, would often send his daughter to the little country store in Hurnville owned and operated by Dan and Louise Oster, both children of Russian immigrants, who both knew about hard work having come from large families who made their living from the good earth. Her family consisted of her parents and nine children who lived in a two-room mud hut made with rock, straw and mud walls with the top made of wood. Dan's family consisted of himself, 8 brothers and sisters, and his parents. After Dan and Louise married in the early 20's they opened their store and operated it for more than 50 years. The store changed little over the years with an old wood and coal burning stove to heat the store, a large counter which once had drawers full of loose crackers, prunes and beans. They used an ornate, antiquated silver cash register to ring up sales. A set of scales set on top of the counter. Old car parts, motor oil, groceries, and general merchandise were found throughout the store. Gasoline was sold from two pumps out front. They provided for the needs of their neighboring farmers, ranchers and cowboys. The store also provided a place for socializing, and Barbara Kafer loved going to that little store.

"Sister, go over to the store and put gas in the truck," Oscar would tell his teenage daughter, and off she would go on farm to market road 1197 to the Oster Store. On arrival she would find one of the Osters behind the counter because they operated the store without the assistance of any employees. They maintained their business continuously throughout the years except, of course, to observe the Sabbath faithfully every Sunday and special holidays, such as Christmas and Thanksgiving. Their days began early at 7:00 a.m. and ended whenever no farmers or ranchers needed any more fuel or additional supplies. On many a day they worked past 7:00 p.m. Twelve hour days were very common, and during harvest, the hours were usually longer. The Osters were examples of business owners who had a strong work ethic and a desire to help others.

Louise raised her children on her hip while she sold groceries, gas and oil. In the early years she also milked a cow twice a day, made butter and cottage cheese and even made the family's clothes just like her mother before her had done. Her husband, Dan, was a very frugal businessman, and Barbara witnessed this on many occasions. She knew the routine that all regular customers had to follow.

Barbara parked the truck next to one of the two gas pumps, then went inside to turn ON the switch which would allow the electricity to operate the pump. Next, she went outside and filled the tank of the truck. While the gas was running, Mr. Oster would occasionally come out to visit, if he was not occupied with another customer inside the store or busy with some chore inside. After filling the tank and replacing the handle into its slot on the pump, she went inside and IMMEDIATELY turned the switch on the electrical outlet to OFF. If one didn't follow this routine to the tee, Mr. Oster's facial expression would easily communicate the need for the customer to comply with his conservative routine. After turning OFF the electricity, Barbara and all customers would walk over to the counter where Mr. Oster would raise his right arm to reach for the string to pull so the light bulb in the ceiling over the front counter could be turned on so he could write the ticket for the customer to sign. After the customer's signature had been written,

Mr. Oster would give the customer the receipt, return the booklet to its appropriate place in the drawer, and reach again to pull the string to turn off the light bulb. On a very sunny day the bulb might not need to be turned on at all.

These folks knew how to "get by" on very little money and no modern conveniences. The old wood and coal burning stove provided heat for the two-room store during the fall and winter seasons. The large stove sat in the northwest corner of the front room of the store. During these colder days, neighbors sometimes gathered around the stove to exchange news of the community and to ponder world affairs. If they stayed long enough, they would sit in the straight back wooden chairs with the slatted seats. The large wooden U-shaped counter in the middle of the floor in the front room, and the floor to ceiling shelves along the walls displayed grocery items, farm supplies and other merchandise.

During warmer days, the farmers and ranchers would sit outside the store where a long wooden plank provided places to sit on either side of the pair of screen doors along the storefront. These visitors often went inside to get something cool to drink and a snack to eat. Inside the store, there was a Coke box to the right of the front doors into which a customer could put coins, lift the lid, and remove a cold drink bottle along the metal track.

Also, a small refrigerator stood to the left of the front door by the edge of the counter. This refrigerator was only turned "on" during the very warmest days of the summer season. The Osters would remove the boxes of candy from the wooden display counter when the daily temperatures began to get hot enough to soften the various candy bars. Inside the refrigerator was this array of boxes of candy bars placed on the metal shelves. On the outside of the refrigerator's single door was taped a piece of white cardboard approximately 12 inches by 18 inches. This sign's information was written in black lettering and read: COLD CANDY 5 CENTS. When a customer wanted to purchase a bar of cold candy from inside the refrigerator, he or she had better not dawdle when making a selection because Mr. Oster did not like to waste money paying a high electricity bill!! If a customer was hesitant in making a decision about which candy bar to purchase, Mr. Oster was sure to give "the look" that told the customer he meant serious business!!

The second room was at the west end of the store. It served mostly as a storage place for tires, oil, farming supplies, and other merchandise. The rear door was where the Osters went to and from their home on the south side of the store. Not much time was spent in the home because the Osters worked so hard inside their store. They took a lot of pride in their store and were quite serious in providing their customers with the best possible service and an adequate selection of groceries and supplies. Everyone in the community worked hard and times were lean. There was very little time for any activities other than hard work for the adults and a combination of school and chores for the children. Saturday evenings and Sundays provided a much needed respite, and a time for socializing. Other opportunities were rare, but one did occur one Halloween evening.

The Moser family lived about a mile north of the Oster Store. A trio of mischievous sons loved nothing more than to pull a prank on some unsuspecting soul. That particular Halloween evening they set their sights on the Oster family. The boys knew the Osters well since they went to school with two Oster daughters and regularly attended Hurnville's only church where the Oster family also were active members. That Halloween night after completing their chores and feeling somewhat frisky, the Moser boys knew that Dan, Louise and the girls would be inside their home fast asleep. They waited until their own parents were slumbering before they crept outside to the barn where the boys collected all of the ropes that were hung on wooden pegs inside the barn door and eased their way south on the road to the Oster Store. It was a clear night with a full moon so their path was easily seen. Upon arriving at the Oster property, they carefully opened the front doors of the

Oster's shed with only a minimal amount of squeaking from the rusty hinges where Dan's prized buckboard was protected from the outside elements. This buckboard was a small, four-wheeled, open carriage with two narrow seats. This was the Oster family's mode of transportation and was faithfully pulled by Nellie for church on Sunday, for visits to neighbors, and rare 10-mile trips to Henrietta.

The boys slowly maneuvered the open buggy out of the shed, closed the shed doors, and pulled it around to the north side of the store away from the house. The ends of each of the four ropes were carefully tied with a double knot to each corner of the buckboard. The eldest boy climbed the tree that had substantial overhanging branches on the store's roof. The loose ends of the ropes were thrown up to him. As the boys on the ground raised the buckboard off the ground and kept it steady, the one on the roof pulled the loose ends to continue the buckboard's upward movement. One more brother scurried up the tree to assist with the pulling. At last, the buckboard was almost even with the roof, so the third "partner in crime" climbed the tree to help secure the buckboard on the roof. Fortunately, the roof had a lower pitch than most buildings its size, so securing the buckboard was not a great challenge. The boys balanced the buckboard as best they could, then proceeded to tie the four loose ends of the ropes to the nearest tree branches on the north and south sides of the roof. Confident that the buckboard was securely balanced in its new location, they climbed down and returned to their home and quietly slipped into their beds for the remainder of the night. You can only imagine the uproar when Dan Oster found his buckboard on the roof of his store the next morning. It was the talk of the town. It didn't take long for the culprits to be identified and amends made by the Mosers. All in all it made for a pretty good laugh, but ole Dan Oster never thought it to be very funny.

The little store in Hurnville is now only a memory. Dan and Louise have passed on but memories of them and their store lingers in the memories of the people like Barbara Kafer. It was the last "gathering place" for farmers, ranchers, cowboys, and neighbors in the once busy community. The last church was the Hurnville Baptist Church, a Northern Baptist affiliate. The church was sold and moved to Wichita Falls, where it continues to be a place of worship. The church's parsonage was purchased by a family and relocated to another community. The small town of Hurnville now stands vacant, but its memories will last forever. Thanks Barbara for your recollections.

XXVI.
"MOVING ALONG"

Aubrey Ramsey was a sad little boy at the age of six when his mother, whom he loved dearly, died in 1925 of an insect bite she sustained while pulling a cotton sack through the cotton patch.

His sister, Beatrice, who was eight years older, took over the role of raising Aubrey for a few years until his father, Dave Ramsey, remarried. As fate would have it, Aubrey did not get along with his stepmother, so in 1934 he went east over a hundred miles down the Red River to Bonham in Fannin County, Texas, where his mother's family lived. He lived with his mother's cousin north of Bonham on his farm in the fertile sandy land of northern Fannin County. Bill Coonrod raised vegetables, strawberries, blackberries and hay.

Cousin Bill had a deal with some stores north of Dallas in McKinney in Collin County to sell them his berries from the farm. Aubrey and his older cousin, Arthur Coonrod, would get an old T-Model Ford with the rear end chopped out and a flat bed laid in, and fill up with berries and head for McKinney some forty miles away. Rolling into Bonham, they would gas up at a store a block to the south of the town square before continuing on to McKinney.

The store in Bonham sold candy, pop and a few groceries. The gas was out front in a glass lined pump about eight feet off the ground. One had to use a hand pump to pump the gas up into the glass lined tank before it was released down into the Model T. There were three pumps. The first pump held white gas, which some called regular, and it sold for 13 cents per gallon. Next there was red gas which was known as ethyl and sold for 14 cents per gallon. The only difference between the two was that red food coloring was added to the ethyl. Then there was lemon crack, which also sold for 14 cents per gallon. It was also white gas with yellow food coloring added, which made it appear green in the overhead glass tank.

After gassing up, Aubrey and his cousin headed on to McKinney where they delivered the berries and took an order for the next week. Sometimes if they had enough extra money that did not belong to Cousin Bill Coonrod, they would stop by a fellow's hot tamale stand on the north edge of McKinney. The hot tamale man, known as Mr. Carpenter, was also known as a breeder of champion fighting chickens, and had the best hot tamales around. He was also rumored to be the purveyor of something a little stronger to drink, which had much appeal to teenage boys like Aubrey. Of course, Aubrey and his cousin could never confirm that rumor about strong drink, but it made for good conversation back in Bonham.

After arriving back in Bonham on their berry runs, Aubrey would go by and see his sister who lived over in the cotton mill section of Bonham as she and her husband worked at the mill. Aubrey was always trying to get his brother-in-law, J. W. Hayes, to go to town and see the doctor. J. W. was in his early 40's, and downtown in an upstairs office on the west side of the square was a doctor named Pruitt. A visit to his office often brought a fee for 50 cents, but with it came a prescription for a pint of whiskey. All one had to do was go over to the south side of the Bonham square on the corner to the drug store and a friendly pharmacist would fill the prescription.

Aubrey had been in the drugstore for years as the F. W. Woolworth store was next door where he had seen his first ceiling fans when he was five. Aubrey was especially fond of his brother-in-law, J. W. Hayes, whom he called Jim because Jim would always give him a nip or two of his Doc Pruitt prescription.

This was life in the south during the great depression of the 1930's and to survive economically Aubrey went to a Civilian Conservation Camp in Arizona, and then to California as President Franklin D. Roosevelt tried to slide the country out of the dire economic grips.

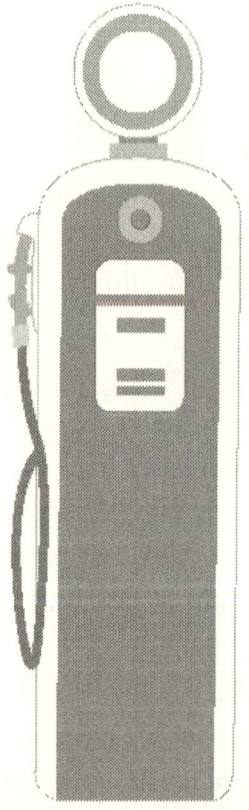

XXVII.
"CHRISTMAS, 1944 AT TERRY LOVE SEVEN"

Aubrey Ramsey had tried to keep his feet on the lineup line as the cold wind blew in his face. It was early February, 1942, and he, like all red blooded American males, was waiting to do his part after the Empire of Japan had bombed Pearl Harbor in Hawaii some two months before. His O.D. field jacket did not break the north wind as the trucks carrying petrol and troops roared up the road next to his basic training company. Aubrey had just recently left the reception station at Fort Sill, Oklahoma, where he thought he had seen the last of standing on lines and in line and waiting. All of Aubrey's time at Fort Sill was just a blur now as he talked to Joe Prasser in the cold in Eastern Belgium almost two years later.

Aubrey's thoughts now were more serious than just his physical comfort. He was wondering if he would be alive a week or month later as the Allied Forces were involved in what he hoped would be the last great battle of World War II in Europe. The German army was making a great push in what was called by some as "The Battle of the Bulge."

Aubrey was called "Doc" because when they were training down in Florida a year earlier, he had picked up a rattlesnake and was milking the venom. He told everyone "this is what we do down in Texas," and so everyone started calling him "Doc" as if he were a snake oil doctor.

Aubrey as a Technician 5th Grade assigned to the 385th Division of the 9th Army Air Force had been on the Continent since June 12, 1944, when he waded ashore in France on Utah Beach at Normandy. The Combat Engineers had cleared a path since the big invasion on June 6, 1944, so that the American GI's would avoid the minefields the Nazis had laid down. Doc had been in England training for several months at Ash Church waiting to go in for the big D-Day invasion.

As he sat in the cold on December 24, 1944, in Eastern Belgium his thoughts wandered back to times in England, especially to the evening at the USO Club at Cheltenham, England, when on a dare from his buddies he wandered over to the other side of the club and asked a young girl to dance. Unfortunately for Doc, he was turned down as the young girl was a princess who would later become Queen Elizabeth II of Great Britain. The princess was polite to this rough GI from Burkburnett, Texas, as she politely said, "I'm sorry, but I am booked up." Doc gracefully nodded and backed away and had a few more of tastes of English bitters.

Corporal Aubrey "Doc" Ramsey was at his forward observation outpost approximately five miles from the Muese River in Eastern Belgium shaking from the morning cold. He and his buddy, Joe Prasser, a school teacher from New Jersey, are one of eight outposts set up this day to watch for German planes and radio back their positions to King High Pole #3, their communications headquarters, who would in turn relay the information to the big anti-aircraft guns which were ready to unload on the enemy planes.

Suddenly Doc's daydreaming is interrupted by an urgent message from headquarters. "Terry Love Seven" this is King High Pole #3, do you read me?" Sergeant William D. Simpson, a Tech 3 radio operator from Florida, is on the sending end. Doc replied, "I read you loud and clear." Suddenly Captain Eugene F. Hunter, the commanding officer yells to Simpson, "Damn it, give me that mike," and screamed, "Hey Doc, the Germans are breaking through up there. Pile up all your equipment, douse it with gasoline, light it with a fire grenade, and you and Prasser get the hell out of there. You're on your own. We can't help you." Doc and Prasser had been dropped off at their outpost by a weapons carrier and were on foot. Their equipment consisted of a field radio, a generator for power, two five gallon jerry cans full of gasoline, binoculars, and their personal weapons. The Germans were about a mile from their position when Doc and Prasser doused the gasoline on the field radio, generator and jerry cans and tossed a fire grenade on the pile. They quickly headed toward the command outpost.

As Doc and Prasser quickly retreated they didn't know that this was the beginning of the "Battle of the Bulge." The last great German offensive of World War II was beginning in earnest and caught the Allies by surprise. When they finally reached the command post on the Muese River over five miles from "Terry Love Seven," everyone was gone, and the bridge across the river had been blown up. Doc and Prasser had no choice but to hide in the basement of an old hotel not far from the blown up bridge and hope and pray that the Germans didn't find them. On Christmas morning they looked out of the small high windows in the basement to see and hear not Germans but Limies in a Model A with machine gun turrets. Doc and Prasser quickly presented themselves to the English Army. "You boys get out of here and get across the river." They swam across the river and were immediately met by British forces manning a machine gun nest. These troops knew that Germans would sometimes put on the uniforms of dead Allied troops and try to infiltrate the lines. These

Limies were taking no chances with Doc and Prasser. They were taken to headquarters and questioned. Doc told them what outfit they were with and what happened and said, "Get on that radio and call our unit. They'll send somebody to ID us and pick us up." Doc and Prasser were held as POW's for about 4 hours until, sure enough, a first lieutenant from their unit arrived and identified them. In the meantime Doc had been processed and given a German POW camp ration book for camp use only for change to buy supplies. It had been issued by the British. The British had also taken away Doc's weapons, a knife and pistol, but these were returned before they headed back by jeep with the first lieutenant to their unit.

Doc and Prasser had eaten nothing but some K-rations for several days and were starving for some hot food. They headed to the chow line, but the mess cook said, "We can't feed you and Prasser because we have orders to feed only 10 men at a time from the front lines." This didn't set too well with Doc and he said "No, me and Prasser are going to eat now or I'll blow you half into." Doc had drawn his 38 British Army pistol. Suddenly, a hand pushed the pistol down. "No Doc, you are not going to kill nobody, but I will if they don't feed you and Prasser," shouted Sergeant Omar R. Persley as he pulled out his 45 and ordered the mess cook to feed those boys.

The mess cook quickly complied and after eating all they wanted, Doc and Prasser reported for duty.

Doc would serve until the end of the war and mustered out on December 5, 1945. He had seen and learned a lot since going into the service of his country on February 5, 1942. From his training state side, to the "buzz bombs" at the big G52 supply depot in England, to the post D-day march across Europe, the great German offensive at the "Battle of the Bulge," to VE Day, and then finally for a ship to return to the states after a five month wait following the war, Aubrey "Doc" Ramsey had served his country honorably just like millions of his fellow soldiers. We owe our freedom to this greatest generation of Americans and their Allied counterparts who defeated the Axis powers.

XXVIII.
"UNCLE J.B."

NOT TOO FAR FROM CORPORAL Aubrey "Doc" Ramsey's forward observation outpost about five miles east of the Muese River in eastern Belgium, the new 84th Infantry Division of the U.S. Army was spending the night near Marche, Belgium, given orders to slow the German 16the Panzer Division. My dad's baby brother, J.B. Balch, was right in the middle of the action. J.B. was a highly decorated enlisted man. On July 11, 1943, his actions as a radio operator in Sicily had won him the Silver Star. Now in Belgium with the newly formed 84th Division he was in a fight to slow this great German offensive. I'll let him tell it in his own words:

"Christmas season of 1944 was a memorable one. The new 84th Infantry Division had only been 'on line' a short time and was still feeling its oats. We had just been sent to the rear for a rest and chance to take showers (canvas enclosures out in the open air with cold-cold-cold temperatures) but the water was warm.

The first night after our arrival in the rest area we were ordered to remove all insignias from clothing and vehicles while preparing to move out immediately.

The Germans had just opened a new desperate offensive to try driving south and then back to the sea thus cutting off several allied divisions. We were to move to the very center of the offensive area and attempt to slow down and disperse the enemy. We traveled all night without lights and arrived somewhere around Marche, Belgium, just before dawn.

We did slow the German 16th Panzer Division, in fact we stalled them thus giving the Allies added time to bring in reserve forces and totally block the enemy offense that proved to be the last German offensive action of the war. The end was near, but some curious things happened during this time frame. For example, on our move forward during the night mentioned above, the Germans in their desperation had dropped parachute troops with excellent command of the English language. They were dressed in U.S. military uniforms with M.P. insignias on their arms. With small flashlights they attempted to direct our convoy in the dark towards their Panzer Divisions, but they were caught and no damage done.

It was a bitter cold day that Christmas of '44 and we had slept out on open ground in our bedrolls a couple or three nights. Each morning we would wake up and scrape the snow away as we were completely covered by a warm blanket of fresh fallen snow. Our greatest fear was that during the night a vehicle would run over us sight unseen. Fortunately that didn't happen.

About the fourth night of this mess my crew found an old barn that looked much more inviting than the open snow fields. The floor was covered with cobble stones, there was a hay rack for cattle to feed from and, indeed, there were a few cattle still occupying the old barn. Before our arrival the Germans had dropped a mortar shell right through the roof and left one huge hole. The stars were clearly visible from that vantage and some snow continued to trickle down through the opening. We dropped to the cobble stone floor as we were due to the utter fatigue and exposure.

It was a beautiful night with the deep snow outside and old Chet (a huge hairy chested fellah from Utah, but a gentle Ben) draped over the hay rack 'Manger'. The only thing disturbing the magic of the night was an occasional artillery shell coming in from the German guns across a couple of ridges from us, or one of ours going out to keep the Germans from sleeping.

About five minutes before midnight that Christmas night a lone enemy plane passed overhead and released a star like flare for artillery to sight our positions. The entire sky lit up and with that snow background. The scene was breathtaking.

I looked up over old Chet in his manger through the hole in the barn's roof and sighted this 'Star of Bethlehem' (actually the enemy flare).

I felt silly holding that wonderful moment to myself or even to dare make such a comparison, but at that instant something wonderful transpired. Our guns ceased fire and the German guns across the hills became silent. For a brief moment friend and foe alike shared a oneness of being and an unmistakable feeling of brotherhood one towards another.

In a few moments the flare died out. The star was extinguished and we were back behaving as humans, but for the first time in over three years of war I felt that those young men across the hills came from homes similar to mine and they had the same deep religious convictions deep down that we so clearly felt.

The war was soon over. We had conquered the enemy. I don't really know what we won, but for those few moments lost in the snowfields of the Battle of the Bulge a lot of young soldiers, American and German, shared something deep and special on Christmas night in 1944."

On December 22, 2003, at the age of 82, we lost Uncle J.B. The last of the Balch brothers was laid to rest in Oak Grove Cemetery in Graham, Texas, on Christmas eve. His brothers, Holt, Judson, and Lemuel, had all crossed over before him, but I truly believe that they welcomed him with open arms into the presence of our Lord. Uncle J.B. and all of his comrades were truly American heroes. According to Jim, his oldest son, Uncle J.B., like a lot of WWII soldiers, never talked much about his war years. With the consent of his family I thought it appropriate to honor him in this book. I could also write about his brothers, Judson and Lemuel, who also served their country during WWII, and Holt, the doctor who served the community back home, but I think they would approve of this tribute to baby brother. Her is his Silver Star Citation in part:

"James B. Balch, #***, Technician Fourth Grade, ****Signal Company, for gallantry in action. At ****, Sicily, on the afternoon of 11 July 1943, as the radio operator on the flagship U.S.S. ***** in ship-to-shore emergency radio net, he was charged with the transmittal and reception of messages vital to the success of the Seventh U.S. Army landing operations at that location. While sending an especially important message pertaining to troop reinforcements, the entire harbor area was subjected to a heavy bombing attack, with shrapnel fragments striking on and near the ship. Although the radio was set up in an exposed position on the fan tail of the ship, Technician Fourth Grade Balch continued transmitting until his messages were completed. His coolness and courage under fire, disregard for personal safety, and devotion to duty reflect the highest traditions of the service. Entered military service from Seymour, Texas."

Uncle J.B. also received the EAME Campaign Medal with six bronze stars, one silver star, and three bronze arrowheads. The bronze and silver stars here were for campaigns and the three arrowheads for invasions. His 1st Amphibian Brigade received the Croix de Guerre from France, which is that nation's highest unit commendation. He volunteered for the Army shortly after Pearl Harbor and served until October 7, 1945. He served in North Africa, Italy, Belgium, and liberated prisoners of war at the Nordhausen Concentration Camp, and was part of the Allied Forces who met the Russians at the Elbe River, Eastern Germany. He was wounded in action and earned the Purple Heart, and received the Silver and Bronze Stars. J. B. was born on September 6, 1921, to Reverend James Robert Balch and Bertha Holt Balch. After graduating from Seymour High School, he enrolled in Decatur Baptist College. After returning to the states, he completed his B.S. at Baylor University and was selected to attend the first series of National Science Foundation Institutes where he received his M.S. from Oklahoma A&M, Stillwater, Oklahoma. He taught high school science at Seymour High School and Levelland High School before joining the faculty at South Plains College. During his 17 years at South Plains College, he received the Excellence in Teaching Award, but his true reward was the joy of working with hundreds of bright and talented students he taught throughout his 35 year teaching career. He is survived by three sons, Jim, Mike and Bill, all medical doctors, his daughter, Candace, who holds a PH.D in education, and his wife, Wanda McCleskey Balch. Uncle J.B. I miss you, and I miss our discussions about our family genealogy. I know you're in a better place, and we'll join you there some day. God Bless You and Your Comrades and May You Rest In Peace.

XXIX.
"BOMBS AWAY"

THE B-17 WAS KNOWN AS the "Flying Fortress" because it had six defensive gun locations, with each location on the fortress holding a 50 caliber machine gun. Second Lieutenant R. G. Fraser's crew and many other similar crews had used up many 9 yard cartridge belts on previous runs, thus giving birth to the phrase "The whole 9 yards." The Nazi fighter planes that they had to dodge and fight sometimes made them wish they had 10 or more yards of cartridge belt. The B-17 was most widely used for daylight strategic bombing of industrial targets. They were compelled to fly in group formation for defensive purposes to allow the Browning 50 calibers of multiple planes to be brought to bear on the enemy fighter planes.

The design of the B-17 was continually improved throughout the war using models B through G in progression. Lt. Fraser's plane named "the tutonic plague" was like the other B-17's in that it could withstand a lot of punishment and still bring the crews back to home base. The Army Air Corps used 12,700 of these great planes built by Boeing and its licensees in the effort to stop Adolph Hitler and the Japanese from 1941 to 1945.

As Second Lieutenant Fraser sat on the runway and looked at the plush farmland to his right, he wondered if the last run of this remarkable B-17 bomber would really be his last. The bomber really shook as all four engines were revving up. The plush farmland of England just did not jive with what he was about to do, but somehow it was made to fit in the tight crevices of his mind.

Since the middle of February, 1945, Lt. Fraser has sat on this same runway with the four big motors idling twenty-six times. Many thoughts ran through his mind when he is in this situation, most of which relate back to his home in central Kansas. This time as the motors rumble, a small hamburger joint in Salina, Kansas, came to mind that sold the Lt. cozy burgers which are small hamburgers that are sold by the dozen in a paper bag. The smell of these cozy burgers filled the cockpit in the mind's eye of Lt. Fraser.

As Lt. Fraser's B-17 comes up to the line to start the taxi to lift off, he sees the top of a farm house to the east and his mind again reverts to the sight of grain elevators outside his hometown of McPherson, Kansas. Suddenly, the signal comes for him to proceed to taxi, and his mind comes back to focus on the runway ahead.

As he gained speed on the smooth English runway, Lt. Fraser wondered, as he always did, why this English runway is always so smooth when the runways where he did his pilot training at Sheppard Field, Wichita Falls, Texas, and bases at Frederick, Oklahoma, and El Reno, Oklahoma, were like rumbling along in a Ford pickup on a gravel road in Western Kansas.

Lt. Fraser always had thoughts when he got close to the end of the English runway if those four powerful motors had the power to lift the fortress off the ground with the two thousand pounds of bombs he was carrying. This is especially true when he considered that the B-17 was carrying 2,700 gallons of fuel on board.

The lieutenant's plane lifted off and as he passed through the clouds he tried to settle back for the four flight to the target at Pilsen, Czechoslovakia, in Bohemia, part of the Nazi war machine. It was April 25, 1945, two days before his mother's birthday, and he had hoped that the war would be over soon. This 27th run was not much different in preparation than his first run back on February 19, 1945.

About three hours after lift off and when things had been remarkably smooth, the AAA (antiaircraft fire) started in somewhere over Germany. After about 10 minutes of dodging the AAA at about 5:00 o'clock, a fast plane appeared and was roaring through the formation when Lt. Fraser's tail gunner radioed him and wanted to know what to do. Lt. Fraser told him to shoot the "SOB" which they all tried to do. However, the plane flying through the formation was one nobody had ever seen because it was one of the first jet aircraft ever seen by an American and had been developed by the German Air Force.

Lt. Fraser was part of the 365th Squadron of the 305th Bomb Group which was part of the 8th Army Air Corp, and the long bombing runs from England with targets in Germany were extremely perilous and mind boggling, but Lt. Fraser and his crew knew that they were really helping the war effort because they could see the destruction of the cities they bombed in Germany from the air. They had hit Berlin twice, Nuremburg twice, Wittenburg, Munich, Dresden and the big industrial city on the North Sea of Hamburg. They had seen the fire and destruction of Hamsburg from 500 miles away on their return trip to England.

The bombing runs where the B-17 carries a lot of fuel like these bombers carry (2,700 gallons of gasoline) scare some pilots and their crew because of the hazards of AAA hitting a fuel tank and the potential for an explosion and fire. Lt. Fraser sometimes tried to quantify exactly how much his B-17 carried in terms of his formative years back in the rural area around his home in McPherson, Kansas. The lieutenant thought a Ford 2N tractor could plow for its entire life for what a B-17 used on one bombing run.

There was one run that Lt. Fraser will never forget and on which he wished the base gasoline station had run a little more petrol in his tank. It all started in the early morning the day after St. Patrick's Day in 1945. Lt. Fraser and his crew were scheduled for a bombing run over Berlin, the capital of Germany, and, hopefully, a target close to the German high command which was barely hanging on in their last days. The run was five hours out and over the English Channel. This was the "tutonic plague's" twelfth run and they all felt like they were a seasoned crew. They had one other run to Berlin back on February 26, 1945, and all had gone smoothly with minimal AAA to contend with. However, as they approached Berlin this time they had to alter their course because of intense AAA and the German fighter planes were attacking from 12 o'clock and 3 o'clock. Lt. Fraser was slightly concerned because the "tutonic plague," although having taken a lot of machine gun fire and flack in the past,, had taken an inordinate amount on this Berlin run.

After the bombs were dropped, the lieutenant noticed that the fuel was a little low and as they made the four hour trip back to England he became very worried.

He did not alarm the crew except that he and his co-pilot were discussing their plans in case they had to ditch in the English Channel or on the beautiful English countryside, as they neared the base south of London. When they reached the base, the sun was low and the gauges on two of the engines showed the fuel tanks were empty, yet the engines were still running. The English countryside, with the sun setting in the west, never looked so good as they hit the runway and rolled on in.

The courage of Lt. Fraser and his crew should always be remembered as a symbol of the sacrifices made by the men and women of the greatest generation who saved our freedoms from the tyranny of the Axis nations of WWII. We owe a large debt of gratitude to the men and women who built, maintained, crewed and piloted the B-17 including Lt. Fraser and his men of the "tutonic plague."

XXX.
"CONCLUSION"

WELL, I'M CAMPING AND TROUT fishing in Colorado about thirty miles behind Pikes Peak in Eleven Mile Canyon with my sons, Trey and Josh, as I write these concluding remarks. This little book has really jogged my memory about growing up in Seymour and of all the people that touched my life. There are many more distributors and operators with their own stories too numerous to elaborate on in these pages. But, I would like to mention some of the distributors and operators that I do remember then and now. Distributors who come to my mind were Frank Keck, Walter Keck, H. F. Harmel, Robert Crowell, Bun Melear, R. L. Moore, Nolan Davis, Joe Tom & John Edd Nelson, Day Carlin, Ron Laney, Jim Richeson, Grozier & Mann, and Phil Davis & Brent Wardlaw. Other operators who come to mind were Cy Bishop, Morris Perkins, Simon Benge, Billy Benge, Randy Benge, Bernie Neatherly, J. T. Duncan, Jimmy Martin, Bun Melear, Nolan Davis, Slugger Smith, Bill Keck, Sam Styles, Jack Richardson, Arthur Jones, Garvin Jones, Hop Parker, A. J. Cooper, Osee Holand, the Easley family Buckhead station, Ferrell Wright, W. J. Roddy, Virgil Bryan, Hubert Thornhill, Bill & Charles Garner, Gene and John Finn Robinson, Tom

& Bill Craddock, Dean Loving, Rick Meaders, Morris Gambrell, Wylie Oil Co., and Jim Lovelace. I know that I have left out many names on this list, but it sure wasn't intentional on my part, and I hope you forgive my failure to include you or your family member.

Seymour was a crossroads town with many stations coming and going thru the years. But, this story can be told in countless towns across America. Pick one, say your hometown. Reach back into the recesses of your memory. Can you see it? The signs, the pumps, the stations, the attendants, their uniforms, do they come to your mind's eye? Now look for the people inside the stations. See their faces. Remember their names. Now make the connection by putting yourself into the picture. These are your gas station stories. Have a few laughs. Talk to old friends about their remembrances. This was America at its finest. Let's never forget this rich history. God bless all of you, and I hope that this little book will rekindle the sparks of remembrance for you as it has for me.

Bob Balch   6/13/05
Eleven Mile Canyon, Colorado

ABOUT THE AUTHOR

Bob Balch is a native Texan who grew up as a Baby Boomer in the Northwest Texas town of Seymour after World War II. He was born in Seymour in 1947 and graduated from Seymour High School in 1965. He then attended Baylor University in Waco, Texas, and graduated with BBA and JD degrees in 1971. He moved to Fort Worth, Texas, and worked for a large multi-national accounting firm for three years. In 1973 he married Debbie Brown, and they moved to Wichita Falls, Texas, in the summer of 1974 where he has practiced law for over 32 years. Bob and Debbie have two sons, Dr. Trey Balch, a physiatry resident at Baylor College of Medicine in Houston, Texas, and Josh, a first year medical student at Ross University on the Eastern Caribbean island of Dominica.

This book "Gas Station Stories" is Bob's fourth published book by AuthorHouse. His previous three books are works of historical fiction. The first book is entitled "The Brazos Connection" and tells the story of a hunter who discovers a great Christian artifact on the Brazos River. The second is entitled "Bridgetown on the Red" and tells the story of two neighbors on the Red River caught up in the great oil boom of 1919. The third is entitled "Treasure of the Wichita" and tells the story of a great treasure buried at the falls of the Wichita River and its discovery by a young Indian woman of the Wichita tribe. This fourth book is nonfiction and is a look at some humorous stories about Bob and his friends growing up in Seymour around gas stations, with some other stories thrown in the mix to spice up the book including some World War II stories as a tribute to this great generation of Americans who saved our country and the freedoms we so enjoy today. Bob hopes this book will both educate, entertain and encourage the reader to reminisce about his or her own experiences with that great American establishment known as the gas station.